ORGANIC CHRISTIANITY

STEVE A. MILLER

SEARCHLIGHT
PUBLICATIONS

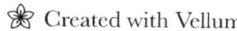

Restore us to yourself, O Lord, that we may be restored! Renew our days as of old— Lamentations 5:21

Contents

Foreword

With keen insight into God's revelation and with clarity of expression, Steve Miller leads his readers into a fresh and invigorating study of the importance of restoring Christianity to the purity with which its Author launched it into the world in the first century. Keying in on the growing popularity of organic foods—foods produced without the use of artificial chemicals, hormones, antibiotics, genetically modified organisms, or additives—the author makes a convincing case for *organic Christianity*—Christianity without the additions and modifications of human opinions, traditions, doctrines, and practices that men have devised and imported into Christianity down through the centuries. A thorough plea is made for pure and simple Christianity free of adulteration and contamination.

The validity of organic Christianity and its importance in today's world is firmly established by the writer of this informative work. He points out that often in our everyday lives we need to have things restored: an iPhone to its original settings, a piece of furniture to its original purpose, a house to its original design, an automobile to its original condition. Demonstrating from the Scriptures how corruption of God's way has repeatedly occurred down through the centuries, appealing to Old Testament examples of apostasy and restoration, the author shows from the New Testament God's original intent for His church and the importance of maintaining that original intent and doing what God said, in the way God said, for the reason God said! The maintenance of the Biblically prescribed way is shown to be applicable both to individual Christians as well as to the church as a whole. The divine side (what God through Christ and the apostles implemented and set forth in the New Testament) is perfect and must never be changed but constantly maintained. Wherein the human side has deviated from, modified, or corrupted the divine side, correction and restoration must take place. As the writer so cogently notes: "Only by adhering to the Divine standard, the Bible, can we be restored individually and collectively as God's people." As he later observes: "When religion has been corrupted, it has to be restored to its original specifications and intent."

The restoration principle—the principle which says that wherein people have departed from God's prescribed way they must return to it—is as old as the fall of humanity into sin and disobedience. Throughout the Scriptures we see the restoration principle at work, the restoration plea being made by courageous men of God, and restoration movements taking place. In this informative book, the author leads us through an investigation of many of these and shows their relevance to our world today. He exalts the Bible as the authoritative pattern to be followed in all things pertaining to Christianity—"the faith which was once for all delivered to the saints" (Jude 3)—and which must be maintained without addition, subtraction, substitution, or modification.

In a day when the teaching of the Bible is little known and little respected, it is important to open that sacred volume and learn from it God's will for mankind. G. K. Wallace, a noted gospel preacher and a respected Bible professor of mine, said many years ago: "The first thing a false teacher wants to do is to get you away from the

Bible." Today, the Bible is reviled and repudiated by many. Its standard of right and wrong is ignored in favor of one's own feelings, emotions, thinking, and the trends of current culture. In compelling fashion, Steve Miller leads his readers to a reverential respect for the Bible as God's pattern for how mankind is to live. As a careful and well-informed student of the Scriptures, he shows that the Bible is the standard for the church in all ages. I predict that *Organic Christianity* will be a worthy and welcomed addition to the body of literature calling for a restoration of the New Testament order of things.

Hugh Fulford
    Gallatin, Tennessee

Introduction

The restoration of New Testament Christianity is a biblical concept. It is rooted in the very nature of our relationship with God.

Each individual must be restored to God due to the separation caused by sin. When this is accomplished, an individual becomes a Christian, a member of the body of Christ. The church must maintain the restoration principle as God created it.

What do we mean when we speak of "the restoration of New Testament Christianity"? Often, individuals will take this to mean that we desire to go back to the 19th Century in belief and practice and are more interested in restoring a 'movement.' The true understanding is that the concept of restoration is a completely biblical topic in both the Old and New Testaments. In the following chapters, we will examine how God is greatly interested in the restoration of the church as He planned, purposed, and established it. He is eternally interested in our personal, individual restoration in order to be in fellowship with Him.

One might ask which New Testament church we are attempting to restore. Some have been cynical and wondered if we might be referring to restoring the congregation at Corinth, Ephesus (Revelation 3:4-5), Pergamum (Revelation 2:14-16), Thyatira (Revelation

3:20-23), Sardis (Revelation 3:1-3), or Laodicea (Revelation 3:15-22). These are examples of churches that had good qualities as well as flaws and sins that God addressed through the writings of the inspired writers. The studious follower of God will quickly comprehend that God is not calling us to restore flaws or sin in ourselves or congregations, but desires us to conform our practices and principles to the standard of His Divine Word (Colossians 3:17). The reality is that due to our human nature, there is no perfect congregation.

Everyone who agrees that one must be a Christian in order to be pleasing to God never entertains that we are calling people to be like Ananias and Sapphira, Alexander or Hymenaeus, Philetus, Demas or Diotrephes (Acts 5:1-4; 1 Timothy 1:19-20; 2 Timothy 2:17-18; 4:10; 3 John 9-10).

The mandate for the restoration of New Testament Christianity is to call people back to Christ in all things.

Restoration is biblical. Restoration is essential. Restoration is ongoing! It is easy to concede that the spirit of restoration is lacking in many churches of Christ. An understanding, application, and proclamation of the restoration principles must be maintained in order to be right with God.

Every generation is responsible for knowing God's way and remaining within it. This involves seeking the truth and owning our faith. At stake is the fact that the church is always one generation away from apostasy (Judges 2:10).

Steve Miller
    Fayetteville, Tennessee

Purpose

The Importance of History

Why is it important for us to know and remember the past? Correct observations have concluded that your view of the future is formed by knowing the past or, in other words, knowing the past can change the future. Great lessons await us in the past that teach, warn, admonish, encourage and guide us in our present relationship with God (Romans 15:4). The restoration of our relationship with God is a major theme throughout the Bible individually and collectively as the church.

Man's History of Departing from God and Returning

One of the greatest illustrations from the Old Testament is Israel's cycle of sin; and stages of servitude, sorrow and salvation.

Sin

The following biblical example traces God's people falling into idolatry.

And the people of Israel did what was evil in the sight of the Lord and served the Baals. And they abandoned the Lord, the God of their fathers, who had brought them out of the land of Egypt. They went after other gods, from among the gods of the peoples who were around them, and bowed down to them. And they provoked the Lord to anger. They abandoned the Lord and served the Baals and the Ashtaroth (Judges 2:11-13).

All Scripture quotations are *English Standard Version* unless otherwise noted.

Servitude

God would then allow other nations to enslave His people where they would serve their enemies.

So the anger of the Lord was kindled against Israel, and he gave them over to plunderers, who plundered them. And he sold them into the hand of their surrounding enemies, so that they could no longer withstand their enemies (Judges 2:14).

Sorrow

The people would eventually respond in sorrow and supplication, pleading for help and relief from their burdens and sin.

Whenever they marched out, the hand of the Lord was against them for harm, as the Lord had warned, and as the Lord had sworn to them. And they were in terrible distress. Then the Lord raised up judges, who saved them out of the hand of those who plundered them. Yet they did not listen to their judges, for they whored after other gods and bowed down to them. They soon turned aside from the way in which their fathers had walked, who had obeyed the commandments of the Lord, and they did not do so. Whenever the Lord raised up judges for them, the Lord was with the judge, and he saved them from the hand of their enemies all the days of the judge. For the Lord was moved to pity by their groaning because of those who afflicted and oppressed them (Judges 2:15-18).

Salvation

In this example, God in His mercy, sends a judge to save them, by bringing them out of the bondage and servitude of their enemies.

But whenever the judge died, they turned back and were more corrupt than their fathers, going after other gods, serving them and bowing down to them. They did not cease their practices or their stubborn ways (Judges 2:19).

Israel made two serious mistakes: First, they did not drive out all the Canannites, leading to the sin of idolatry (Judges 1:28; 2:12). Second, they did not teach their children about God and His great acts of deliverance.

The cycle occurred seven times in the book of Judges.

Othniel (3:7-11).

Ehud/Shamgar (3:12-31).

Deborah (4:1-5:31).

Gideon (6:1-8:28).

Tola/Jair (10:1-5).

Jephthah (10:6-12:7).

Samson (13:1-16:31).

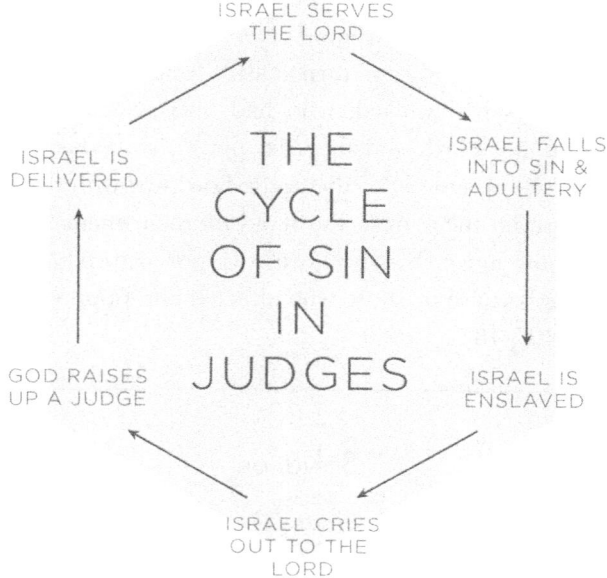

Are we any different today? We follow the same progression in our lives. Man becomes enslaved to sin leading him away from God (1 John 1:6,8; Romans 3:23). When man "comes to himself" (Luke 15:17) (acknowledges the sin and departure from God in his life and returns to God), God is ready to accept and forgive him.

We repent, confess the name of Christ and are baptized into Christ for the remission of sins (1 John 1:9), and experience deliverance from the progression of sin (1 John 1:7).

The importance of instructing our children and new disciples in the teachings of being restored is echoed in the tragic statement, "And there arose another generation after them who did not know the Lord or the work that he had done for Israel" (Judges 2:10).

Four Realities in the Ideology of Restore

The Church Pre-existed Before the Reformation Movement

The term Protestant was "first used at the Diet of Speyer in 1529 by Lutherans who wished to offer "protest" to the decisions of the Roman Catholic Church" (George A. Mather and Larry A. Nichols, *Dictionary Of Cults, Sects, Religions And The Occult.* Grand Rapids: Zondervan, 1993, 224).

Denominationalism was the result of the Reformation Movement. The seeds, however, were sown for future individuals to strive to take the Word of God as their only rule of faith and practice. All Protestant denominations were founded hundreds of years after Pentecost in Acts chapter 2. The churches of Christ are not a Protestant denomination. The church pre-dates the Reformation Movement.

The Church Pre-existed Before the Restoration Movement

"Now the Spirit expressly says that in later times some will depart from the faith" (1 Timothy 4:1). The propagation of human creeds that were believed and practiced led people into the abyss of ignorance regarding spiritual matters. This provided an opportunity for those seeking restoration of New Testament Christianity, having been a part of various denominational groups, to work toward restoring the New Testament pattern, rejecting human creeds and traditions that had long divided the religious world. "We will speak where the Bible speaks and be silent where the Bible is silent," meaning, there must be Bible authority for what is practiced in religion. They realized the seriousness of changing God's word (Matthew 15:9; Galatians 1:6-9). No one of the restoration movement in the 19th century established the church of Christ. The church pre-dates the Restoration Movement.

The Church Pre-existed Before Denominationalism

The third reality involves the fact the church existed before man-made denominationalism.

Denominationalism has been described in the following fashion:

The system and ideology founded on the division of the religious population into numerous ecclesiastical bodies, each stressing particular values or traditions and each competing with the other in the same community under substantial conditions of freedom (Jerald C. Brauer, Ed., *The Westminster Dictionary of Church History*, Philadelphia: The Westminster Press, 1971, 262-263.

The definition highlights several weaknesses of denominationalism when examined in the light of the Scriptures. Division is a hallmark of the denominational conglomeration. The dividing into separate organizations is condemned in the Bible (1 Corinthians 1:10). The Word of God teaches there is only one body, the church (Romans 12:4-5). Sound doctrine is promoted by God (Titus 2:1) and the idea that there is a freedom to differ on "one Lord, one faith, one baptism," etc., is nowhere found in the teaching of the New Testament. It is not up to men to decide on what is faith or practice, but Christ who is the head of the church and has all authority (Ephesians 1:22).

The Bible speaks against denominationalism in the following ways:

It promotes division (1 Corinthians 1:10).

It redefines the Church (Ephesians 5:23-24).

It denies the importance of the Church (Acts 20:28).

It consents to the choices of men above the Word of God (Jeremiah 10:23).

It is built upon man's sincerity rather than God's Truth (Acts 23:1).

It ignores the divine standard of unity (John 17:17).

It approves making laws where God has not made them (Galatians 1:6-9).

Denominations have never been part of God's plan for the church.

The following questions are relevant in the discussion of Scripture teaching and the existence of denominations:

1. Were the apostles members of a denomination?
2. Was the church Jesus established a denomination?
3. Is it possible to be a Christian today without belonging to any denomination?
4. Must one belong to (any) denomination in order to be saved?
5. Must one belong to (any) denomination in order to live the Christian life?
6. Must one belong to (any) denomination in order to go to Heaven?
7. Is it possible today to be a member of the church Jesus established?
8. Must one belong to the Lord's church in order to be saved?
9. Must one belong to the Lord's church in order to live the Christian life?
10. Must one belong to the Lord's church in order to go to Heaven?

A man can do everything the Bible teaches him to do to be saved and never be a member of a denomination. However, he has to do something in addition to, or instead of, what the Bible teaches to be a member of a denomination. From Pentecost on, no person in the Bible was ever saved outside of Christ's church, and in the

Bible, no saved person was ever added by the Lord to any denomination.

Exposing the fact that denominationalism has no authority or right to exist is because of:

Its system,

Its principles,

Its doctrines,

Its organization, or

Its aims.

It is not about the people. It is about the existence of denominations in their form as a perversion of God's plan for the church. Denominationalism is a human view of the church which condones and encourages differing church organizations.

Denominations have earthly headquarters and operate by their own sets of rules and authority. The existence of the denominational structure, hierarchy, and practice is unnecessary for the existence of Christianity. It is unnecessary for any spiritual blessing (Acts 2; 2 Peter 1:3), and it is unnecessary in Christian worship and the church's work.

The church of Christ is not a denomination (Matthew 16:18; Ephesians 1:22-23; 4:4; John 17:20-21; Acts 20:28; 2:41, 47; Ephesians 5:25).

The Church of Christ existed before denominationalism. Membership in the church is NOT optional for a Christian.

The church is essential to our salvation. If you are not in the church, then you are not a Christian. We often hear statements like the following:

"One does not have to be a member of the church to be saved."

"The church doesn't save anyone."

"One can be a Christian and not be a member of any church."

Let's consider three questions that bring the issue into focus.

First, **who is the Savior of mankind** (Acts 4:12)?

Second, **when is a man saved?** When he obeys the gospel (Mark 16:16).

Third, **where does Christ save?** (Ephesians 5:23; Colossians 1:18).

Now let's examine: **Where is salvation?** In the church of the Lord. **Who saves?** Christ. **When?** When we obey His Gospel. Paul declares that Christ is the Savior of the body, the church (Ephesians 5:23). One must be a member of that of which Christ is the Savior in order to be saved (1 Corinthians 15:24). Since the church is the body of Christ, and Christ is the Savior of the body, then one cannot be saved and not be a member of the church. The church of Christ is not the Savior, it is the saved. All who are saved from past sins are in the church, or the saved make up the church. To be saved is to be in Christ - salvation is in Christ. To be saved equals being in the church, the Lord adds you when you are saved (Acts 2:47). To be in Christ is to be in His church.

The church is Christ's. It is built on Him. Bought by His blood. Ruled by His Will. Sustained by His power.

The church of Christ is the one body of Jesus Christ (Colossians 1:18; Ephesians 4:4). Through history, the blood-bought church has endured countless persecutions and has weathered the onslaughts of Satan in every age. The church has survived. It shall never be destroyed (Daniel 2:44). The seed is the word of God (Luke 8:11), and where it is planted and watered, Christians will be produced (Acts 2:38, 47).

What Restoring Is Not

The sections in this book are written to remind us of what is involved in efforts to restore ourselves to God, as well as being the church that He purposed, and that Jesus shed His blood to purchase as "the assembly of the firstborn" (Hebrews 12:23).

Before we undertake the task of outlining the restoration principle, let us briefly review what the restoration principle does not involve.

1. It is not seeking to establish a new church.
2. It is not to reform a church, its practices, or its organizational structure.
3. It is not to restore the faults or sins in the lives of New Testament members (Ex: Ananias and Sapphira).
4. It is not an effort to restore the customs and culture of the first century.
5. It is not an effort to restore the spiritual gifts (1 Corinthians 12:4-11; 13:8-12; John 20:30-31) of the first century.
6. It is not a call to ecumenicism (a false, non-biblical unity fellowship that seeks to unite all denominations…a movement that promotes worldwide unity among all religions through greater cooperation, see Galatians 1:6-9).
7. It is not an effort to restore the sinful practices held by members of some of the New Testament congregations.
8. It is not a restoring of an American church born in the nineteenth century. The New Testament church was not born in the eighteenth or nineteenth century in America. It began on the first Pentecost after the resurrection of Christ recorded in Acts chapter two.
9. It is not based upon any preacher, theological doctrine, editor, periodical, or school.
10. It is not to accept any theological teaching originated by any denomination, individual, council, or synod.
11. It is not designed to bind anything on any individual or group which is a matter of human tradition (Matthew 16:19).

12. It is not to refuse to re-examine any teaching in the light of God's Word.

Misconceptions have existed in the minds of many people over time necessitating a continual revisiting of the true biblical principles that involve the restoration of New Testament Christianity in each generation.

Pure

Finally, brothers, whatever is true, whatever is honorable, whatever is just, whatever is pure, whatever is lovely, whatever is commendable, if there is any excellence, if there is anything worthy of praise, think about these things (Philippians 4:8).

God's Original Intent

Purity is the idea of freedom from adulteration or contamination. We desire purity in the water we drink and the food we eat. This extends into many areas in our lives. Being free from contamination and perversion should also be desired in our religious devotion to the God of Creation.

A word widely used today is "organic." "Organic" is generally described as being without any additives (of food or farming methods) produced or involving production without the use of chemical fertilizers, pesticides, or other artificial agents. The billion-dollar organic industry prides itself on being absent of modern synthetic inputs such as pesticides and chemical fertilizers. Other characteristics include the lack of antibiotics, artificial colors, or genetically modified ingredients.

A correlation between the idea of the organic nature and the purity of New Testament Christianity exists. Pure Christianity could be described as "organic" in the sense that it was and is formed without any additives or artificial teachings of man and occurs when an individual comes in contact with the Scriptures and develops an obedient faith (Acts 22:16) in God and Jesus Christ.

Purity of doctrine results from recognizing Christ as the only authority for our faith and practice. This realization will cause adherence to the teaching of Christ in the New Testament. "Everyone who goes on ahead and does not abide in the teaching of Christ, does not have God. Whoever abides in the teaching has both the Father and the Son. If anyone comes to you and does not bring this teaching, do not receive him into your house or give him any greeting, for whoever greets him takes part in his wicked works" (2 John 9-11). The Apostle Paul instructs: "that you may learn by us not to go beyond what is written" (1 Corinthians 4:6), and he revealed to Timothy, "Keep a close watch on yourself and on the teaching" (1 Timothy 4:16). This is in keeping with the warnings of Jesus when He said, "For false christs and false prophets will arise and perform signs and wonders, to lead astray, if possible, the elect" Mark 13:22) and, "Beware of false prophets, who come to you in sheep's clothing but inwardly are ravenous wolves. You will recognize them by their fruits" (Matthew 7:15-16).

Our Lord and His apostles recognized the importance of keeping the teaching pure, with no additives or modifications, whatsoever. It is also clear that we can know the truth and recognize false teaching when we come into contact with it (John 8:32; Matthew 7:20). God has left us with the Inspired Word that gives us the standard to measure all things and a point of reference to return to when we fall away.

Let us now define the word *restore* and develop three pre-suppositions that must be acknowledged.

Presupposes

Have you ever needed to restore your iPhone to its original settings due to some form of corruption? If so, you have conducted a restoration. In our world, restoration is a common word and concept that signifies a return to the original specifications as given by the designer at the beginning. Costly research is conducted for detailed plans and blueprints to discover what was the original pattern for furniture, historic houses, buildings, automobiles, or anything built or manufactured. For example, an automobile restoration is defined as an automobile that has been rebuilt exactly the way its manufacturer first assembled it at the factory. In other words, it goes back to its default, original specifications, and condition.

Can the model of restoring be applied religiously? Biblically? Yes!

Let's define some terms.

Restore: To give back (something taken away, lost, etc.); make restitution of. To bring back to a former or normal condition, as by repairing, rebuilding, altering, etc.; to put back in a place, position, rank, etc (*Webster's New World College Dictionary*, Fourth Edition, Cleveland: Wiley Publishing, Inc. 2010, 1222).

Bring back (a previous right, practice, custom, or situation); reinstate...return (someone or something) to a former condition, place, or position...repair or renovate (a building, work of art, vehicle, etc.) so as to return it to its original condition (*Webster's*, 1222).

The noun "**restoration**" is:

"a restoring or being restored; specify., a) reinstatement in a former position, rank, etc. b) restitution for loss, damage, etc., c) a putting or bringing back into a former, normal, or unimpaired state or condition" (Webster's, 1222).

Carefully notice the terms in these definitions: to bring back; to put back in place; return; to its original condition; normal or unimpaired state or condition.

The contents of these meanings of restoration can be succinctly presented:

To repair and reset the pattern in the current generation by faithfully returning and adhering to the Word of God. This will involve removing deficiencies and anything not intended by the original designer. This mandate will require the Christian to reawaken the desire to set back in place the original plan as purposefully given by God in His Word which is accomplished by humbly dedicating ourselves to the restoring of God's way for the church and our individual lives. We must always remember that departing (falling away) from God's standard is always possible and maintaining sound doctrine is the objective in order to remain in God's favor (*Steve A. Miller*)

Reformation

A line of distinction must be made recognizing that restoration is not reformation.

"Reformation" is defined as: "To make better by removing faults and defects; correct. To make better by putting a stop to abuses or malpractices, or by introducing better procedures, etc" (*Webster's*, 1204).

The Reformation movement was by its design a means of only reforming Catholicism. Tragically, the leaders of the reformation movement of the sixteenth century did not go all the way back to Jerusalem, Acts chapter two. Making some corrections and trying to clean up some corruption is not synonymous with restoring.

It could be implied that the reformation helped influence the mindset and sow seed for future individuals to see the persistent need to go completely back to the New Testament and restore (put back in its original condition) the church of the New Testament. In time, men realized that what was needed was not reformation but restoration. "Restore us to yourself, O Lord, that we may be restored! Renew our days as of old" (Lamentations 5:21).

Three Basic Traits

To arrive at the proper understanding and practice of restoration, there are three basic traits to consider:

An open Bible. The availability of the Scriptures and the freedom to read them helped spread the fires of reformation. The same characteristics fueled and gave vision to the ideal of ongoing restoration. An open Bible is a necessary ingredient in the process of restoration. The Bible shows the way (Psalm 119:105) and makes Christians only (Acts 11:26). It has also given us the church (Luke 8:11; Acts 2:38, 47). Without the Scriptures, restoration is impossible.

We must embrace the example of the Bereans in order to be restored: "Now these Jews were more noble than those in Thessalonica; they received the word with all eagerness, examining the Scriptures daily to see if these things were so" (Acts 17:11).

An open heart. A heart that is led by the Word of God will be receptive to the Will of God and will desire to be right with God. In the long ago, God relayed to Jeremiah a message for Israel that was repeated in the New Testament: "For this is the covenant that I will make with the house of Israel after those days, declares the Lord: I will put my law within them, and I will write it on their hearts. And I will be their God, and they shall be my people" (Jeremiah 31:33; Hebrews 8:10). A heart and mind filled with the Word will serve us in seeking to be faithful in our relationship with God:

"Let the word of Christ dwell in you richly, teaching and admonishing one another in all wisdom, singing psalms and hymns and spiritual songs, with thankfulness in your hearts to God" (Colossians 3:16). "Then I said, "Behold, I have come; in the scroll of the book it is written of me: I delight to do your will, O my God; your law is within my heart" (Psalm 40:7-8).

A lady by the name of Lydia serves this point as a great example: "One who heard us was a woman named Lydia, from the city of Thyatira, a seller of purple goods, who was a worshiper of God. The Lord opened her heart to pay attention to what was said by Paul" (Acts 16:14). Lydia demonstrated a receptive heart and spirit. "So faith comes from hearing, and hearing through the word of Christ" (Romans 10:17).

Paul commended the Thessalonians for having a prepared, accepting response to the Word they were proclaiming: "And we also thank God constantly for this, that when you received the word of God, which you heard from us, you accepted it not as the word of men but as what it really is, the word of God, which is at work in you believers" (1 Thessalonians 2:13).

A Submissive Soul Resulting in Obedience. An open Bible and a receptive heart should lead to an obedient response to the received teaching. When Philip came upon the nobleman who was returning from Jerusalem, who was reading Isaiah chapter fifty-three, the Ethiopian became convinced by Philip of Jesus Christ being the suffering servant who died for all and desired to complete his belief of obedience:

And the eunuch said to Philip, "About whom, I ask you, does the prophet say this, about himself or about someone else?" Then Philip opened his mouth, and beginning with this Scripture he told him the good news about Jesus. And as they were going along the road they came to some water, and the eunuch said, "See, here is water! What prevents me from being baptized?" And he commanded the chariot to stop, and they both went down into the water, Philip and the eunuch, and he baptized him. And when they came up out of the water, the Spirit of the Lord carried Philip away, and the eunuch saw him no more, and went on his way rejoicing (Acts 8:34-39).

God has always required an obedient response to His commands which is required in order to receive His promises (Genesis 6:5-7; Leviticus 10:1-3; Mark 16:16).

Apostasy, An Authoritative Standard and Aspiration

We will now study the fact that restoration presupposes at least three things: 1. apostasy, 2. an authoritative standard, and 3. an aspiration to return to the standard of God's Word.

For restoration to be existent, there must be corruption or a departure from the original plan. A standard is necessary to know when one has moved away from the original intent and thus provides a plan and point of return. In order to accomplish this in any situation, there must be a willingness, a desire, to go back and restore the original.

Apostasy

Going back to the default, original position, in any endeavor reminds us that there must have been changes, corruptions, deteriorations, and modifications over time in order to warrant a restoration.

God has always provided His Word which has detailed boundaries, landmarks, and a framework for where He expects His people to abide, worship and serve. It is a grave error to forsake the pattern God has originated in any generation.

Abandoning the landmarks of God results in apostasy. Apostasy is defined as: "defiance of established system or authority, rebellion, abandonment, breach of faith." (William Arndt et al., *A Greek-English Lexicon of the New Testament and Other Early Christian Literature.* Chicago: University of Chicago Press, 2000, 120). Any time God's people abandon the truth, they forfeit fellowship with God and provoke His wrath against them. Hosea, who ministered to the northern kingdom of Israel who was steeped in moral corruption and spiritual adultery, stated: "The princes of Judah have become like those who move the landmark; upon them I will pour out my wrath like water" (Hosea 5:10). God is not pleased when men move, change, or abandon His boundaries that serve as identifying marks.

Falling Away

When corruption and falling away occur, there is a need to return to a faithful relationship with God. Throughout the Scriptures, there have been warnings of failing to live up to God's arrangement.

Adam and Eve (Genesis 3) fell away from God's commandment. Cain fell short in his sacrifice (Genesis 4). The generation of Noah rebelled (Genesis 6). The descendants of Noah failed and disobeyed (Genesis 9-11). After being freed from Egyptian bondage, the generation went against God and His commands (Exodus 14-32). After Joshua, the generation went into a cycle of apostasy and restoration (Judges 2:10-23). Jeroboam, who changed and corrupted God's commands in the realm of worship, serves as an evil example: "So the king took counsel and made two calves of gold. And he said to the people, "You have gone up to Jerusalem long enough. Behold your gods, O Israel, who brought you up out of the land of Egypt" (1 Kings 12:28).

God removed the Israelite tribes of the north because of corruption (2 Kings 17). The southern tribe of Judah suffered the same conclusion (2 Chronicles 36). In the books of Malachi (1-2) and Ezra (9-10), those that returned from captivity proved they had not learned their lessons.

New Testament Warnings

Departing from the faith is real. The following references serve as illustrations of multiple warnings and are representative and not exhaustive in the New Testament.

- Beware of false prophets, who come to you in sheep's clothing but inwardly are ravenous wolves. You will recognize them by their fruits. Are grapes gathered from thornbushes, or figs from thistles (Matthew 7:15-16)?

- For false christs and false prophets will arise and perform signs and wonders, to lead astray, if possible, the elect (Mark 13:22).

- And the ones on the rock are those who, when they hear the word, receive it with joy. But these have no root; they believe for a while, and in time of testing fall away (Luke 8:13).

- After this many of his disciples turned back and no longer walked with him (John 6:66).

- I know that after my departure fierce wolves will come in among you, not sparing the flock; and from among your own selves will arise men speaking twisted things, to draw away the disciples after them. Therefore be alert, remembering that for three years I did not cease night or day to admonish every one with tears (Acts 20:29-31).

- I appeal to you, brothers, to watch out for those who cause divisions and create obstacles contrary to the doctrine that you have been taught; avoid them. For such persons do not serve our Lord Christ, but their own appetites, and by smooth talk and flattery they deceive the hearts of the naive (Romans 16:17-18).

- I appeal to you, brothers, by the name of our Lord Jesus Christ, that all of you agree, and that there be no divisions among you, but that you be united in the same mind and the same judgment. For it has been reported to me by Chloe's people that there is quarreling among you, my brothers (1 Corinthians 1:10-11).

- I am astonished that you are so quickly deserting him who called you in the grace of Christ and are turning to a different gospel— not that there is another one, but there are some who trouble you and want to distort the gospel of Christ. But even if we or an angel from heaven should preach to you a gospel contrary to the one we preached to you, let him be accursed. As we have said before, so now I say again: If anyone is preaching to you a gospel contrary to the one you received, let him be accursed (Galatians 1:6-9).

- So that we may no longer be children, tossed to and fro by the waves and carried about by every wind of doctrine, by human cunning, by craftiness in deceitful schemes (Ephesians 4:14).

- For many, of whom I have often told you and now tell you even with tears, walk as enemies of the cross of Christ. Their end is destruction, their god is their belly, and they glory in their shame, with minds set on earthly things (Philippians 3:18-19).

- I say this in order that no one may delude you with plausible arguments (Colossians 2:4).

- See to it that no one takes you captive by philosophy and empty deceit, according to human tradition, according to the elemental spirits of the world, and not according to Christ (Colossians 2:8).

- For they themselves report concerning us the kind of reception we had among you, and how you turned to God from idols to serve the living and true God, and to wait for his Son from heaven, whom he raised from the dead, Jesus who delivers us from the wrath to come (1 Thessalonians 1:9-10).

- But test everything; hold fast what is good. Abstain from every form of evil (1 Thessalonians 5:21-22).

- Let no one deceive you in any way. For that day will not come, unless the rebellion comes first, and the man of lawlessness is revealed, the son of destruction, who opposes and exalts himself against every so-called god or object of worship, so that he takes his seat in the temple of God, proclaiming himself to be God. Do you not remember that when I was still with you I told you these things? And you know what is restraining him now so that he may be revealed in his time. For the mystery of lawlessness is already at work. Only he who now restrains it will do so until he is out of the way. And then the lawless one will be revealed, whom the Lord Jesus will kill with the breath of his mouth and bring to nothing by the appearance of his coming. The coming of the lawless one is by the activity of Satan with all power and false signs and wonders, and with all wicked deception for those who are perishing, because they refused to love the truth and so be saved. Therefore God sends them a strong delusion, so that they may believe what is false, in order that all may be condemned who did not believe the truth but had pleasure in unrighteousness (2 Thessalonians 2:3-12).

- Holding faith and a good conscience. By rejecting this, some have made shipwreck of their faith, among whom are Hymenaeus and Alexander, whom I have handed over to Satan that they may learn not to blaspheme (1 Timothy 1:19-20).

- Now the Spirit expressly says that in later times some will depart from the faith by devoting themselves to deceitful spirits and teachings of demons, through the insincerity of liars whose consciences are seared, who forbid marriage and require abstinence from foods that God created to be received with thanksgiving by those who believe and know the truth (1 Timothy 4:1-3).

- And their talk will spread like gangrene. Among them are Hymenaeus and Philetus, who have swerved from the truth, saying that the resurrection has already happened. They are upsetting the faith of some (2 Timothy 2:17-18).

- But understand this, that in the last days there will come times of difficulty (2 Timothy 3:1).

- Just as Jannes and Jambres opposed Moses, so these men also oppose the truth, men corrupted in mind and disqualified regarding the faith (2 Timothy 3:8).

- Preach the word; be ready in season and out of season; reprove, rebuke, and exhort, with complete patience and teaching. For the time is coming when people will not endure sound teaching, but having itching ears they will accumulate for themselves teachers to suit their own passions, and will turn away from listening to the truth and wander off into myths (2 Timothy 4:2-4).

- My brothers, if anyone among you wanders from the truth and someone brings him back...(James 5:19).

- For there are many who are insubordinate, empty talkers and deceivers, especially those of the circumcision party. They must be silenced, since they are upsetting whole families by teaching for shameful gain what they ought not to teach (Titus 1:10-11).

- Therefore we must pay much closer attention to what we have heard, lest we drift away from it. For since the message declared by angels proved to be reliable, and every transgression or disobedience received a just retribution, how shall we escape if we neglect such a great salvation (Hebrews 2:1-3)?

- Take care, brothers, lest there be in any of you an evil, unbelieving heart, leading you to fall away from the living God (Hebrews 3:12).

- For it is impossible, in the case of those who have once been enlightened, who have tasted the heavenly gift, and have shared in the Holy Spirit, and have tasted the goodness of the word of God and the powers of the age to come, and then have fallen away, to restore them again to repentance, since they are crucifying once again the Son of God to their own harm and holding him up to contempt (Hebrews 6:4-6).

- For it is time for judgment to begin at the household of God; and if it begins with us, what will be the outcome for those who do not obey the gospel of God? And "If the righteous is scarcely saved, what will become of the ungodly and the sinner?" Therefore let those who suffer according to God's will entrust their souls to a faithful Creator while doing good (1 Peter 4:17-19).

- Be sober-minded; be watchful. Your adversary the devil prowls around like a roaring lion, seeking someone to devour. Resist him, firm in your faith, knowing that the same kinds of suffering are being experienced by your brotherhood throughout the world. And after you have suffered a little while, the God of all grace, who has called you to his eternal glory in Christ, will himself restore, confirm, strengthen, and establish you (1 Peter 5:8-10).

- But false prophets also arose among the people, just as there will be false teachers among you, who will secretly bring in destructive heresies, even denying the Master who bought them, bringing upon themselves swift destruction. And many will follow their sensuality, and because of them the way of truth will be blasphemed. And in their greed they will exploit you with false words. Their condemnation from long ago is not idle, and their destruction is not asleep (2 Peter 2:1-3).

- As he does in all his letters when he speaks in them of these matters. There are some things in them that are hard to understand, which the ignorant and unstable twist to their own destruction, as they do the other Scriptures. You therefore, beloved, knowing this beforehand, take care that you are not carried away with the error of lawless people and lose your own stability (2 Peter 3:16-17).

- Children, it is the last hour, and as you have heard that antichrist is coming, so now many antichrists have come. Therefore we know that it is the last hour. They went out from us, but they were not of us; for if they had been of us, they would have continued with us. But they went out, that it might become plain that they all are not of us (1 John 2:18-19).

- Beloved, do not believe every spirit, but test the spirits to see whether they are from God, for many false prophets have gone out into the world (1 John 4:1).

- For many deceivers have gone out into the world, those who do not confess the coming of Jesus Christ in the flesh. Such a one is the deceiver and the antichrist (2 John 7).

- Everyone who goes on ahead and does not abide in the teaching of Christ, does not have God. Whoever abides in the teaching has both the Father and the Son. If anyone comes to you and does not bring this teaching,

26

do not receive him into your house or give him any greeting (2 John 9-10).

- For certain people have crept in unnoticed who long ago were designated for this condemnation, ungodly people, who pervert the grace of our God into sensuality and deny our only Master and Lord, Jesus Christ (Jude 4).

- But you must remember, beloved, the predictions of the apostles of our Lord Jesus Christ. They said to you, "In the last time there will be scoffers, following their own ungodly passions" (Jude 17-18).

- Remember therefore from where you have fallen; repent, and do the works you did at first. If not, I will come to you and remove your lampstand from its place, unless you repent (Revelation 2:5).

- I warn everyone who hears the words of the prophecy of this book: if anyone adds to them, God will add to him the plagues described in this book, and if anyone takes away from the words of the book of this prophecy, God will take away his share in the tree of life and in the holy city, which are described in this book (Revelation 22:18-19).

Observations

Departures were predicted by the inspiration of the Holy Spirit.

False teaching exists.

False teachers are real.

False teaching and teachers can be identified.

Apostasy is gradual.

There is a standard to judge everything.

God desires our return when we stray.

Individuals can fall away.

Congregations can fall away (Revelation 2:1-7; 2 Thessalonians 2:3).

God will forgive us when we return.

God demands faithfulness to Him and His Word.

We can watch and guard against being deceived and falling away.

God's wrath is upon those who pervert his teachings.

Some who obey will leave Christ and go back into the world.

False teachers often come from within.

Those who cause divisions are selfish.

God expects unity in the church.

We must know the Word in order to test the teachings of man.

The devil is behind all false teachings.

Fellowship with God is forfeited when we remain outside the doctrine of Christ.

False teachers are deceptive.

Rejection of the Ancient Paths

"Thus says the Lord: "Stand by the roads, and look, and ask for the ancient paths, where the good way is; and walk in it, and find rest for your souls. But they said, 'We will not walk in it'" (Jeremiah 6:16). Jeremiah found that the people were immersed in their sins and abandoned God's Will in their lives and religious devotion.

Tragically, illustrations abound where man has continued to have the attitude of "we will not walk" in the Will of God. This is evident in human teachings, practices, opinions, and creeds.

In the New Testament, the Apostle Paul found the church in Corinth divided over men. This was less than ten years since Pentecost (Acts 2). "I appeal to you, brothers, by the name of our Lord Jesus Christ, that all of you agree, and that there be no divisions among you, but that you be united in the same mind and the same judgment. For it has been reported to me by Chloe's people that there is quarreling among you, my brothers" (1 Corinthians 1:10-11). Paul rebuked them and reminded them: "For no one can lay a foundation other than that which is laid, which is Jesus Christ. Let no one deceive himself. If anyone among you thinks that he is wise in this age, let him become a fool that he may become wise" (1 Corinthians 3:11, 18). To the churches of Galatia, Paul expressed God's displeasure at their departures: "But even if we or an angel from heaven should preach to you a gospel contrary to the one we preached to you, let him be accursed. As we have said before, so now I say again: If anyone is preaching to you a gospel contrary to the one you received, let him be accursed" (Galatians 1:8-9).

The end result is that we need to come back to God as a church and restore the practices and principles to His Will in order to be right with Him. We must restore both sides. The Divine side is perfect, and must be implemented and maintained, needing no revision, human addition or subtraction. The human side is flawed and is in need of constant work in the form of repentance and restoration. There are things in our lives and in our congregations that we must put to death. "Now the works of the flesh are evident: sexual immorality, impurity, sensuality, idolatry, sorcery, enmity, strife, jealousy, fits of anger, rivalries, dissensions, divisions, envy, drunkenness, orgies, and things like these. I warn you, as I warned you before, that those who do such things will not inherit the kingdom of God" (Galatians 5:19-21). There are good traits that need to be supplied as well, "But the fruit of the Spirit is love, joy, peace, patience, kindness, goodness, faithfulness, gentleness, self-control; against such things there is no law" (Galatians 5:22-23).

Let us now examine the standard that God has given to know the truth and abide by it.

Authority

There must be in everything an accepted standard, a source of final authority.

In everyday terms of use, we might reference a yardstick for measuring, scales for weighing, or a monetary system for evaluating. The dictionary settles questions of pronunciation and word usage; mathematics has its rules and methods relating to quantities, magnitudes and operations; corporations have their charters and by-laws; states have their statutes; nations have their constitutions.

Christianity is the religion of Divine authority. To be pleasing to God, man must be submissive to God's will for him. It should not, therefore seem strange that God has a standard of measuring right and wrong. Authority is needed to give the right to act (Acts 26:10).

In order for society to function smoothly, authority is required. Authority is at the basis of responsibility. The Jews correctly asked Jesus: "Tell us by what authority you do these things, or who it is that gave you this authority" (Luke 20:2). Authority here means: **"the right to control or command, *authority*, *absolute power*, *warrant*"** (William Arndt et al., *A Greek-English Lexicon*, 353).

The fact that Jesus' teaching was passed on through His inspired apostles to teachers of the Word meant they had a standard by which to measure the actions of other people. Without such a standard, sin found in our lives could not be called into question and corrected, and evildoers could not be rebuked and reproved! The church would be lost in confusion and corruption in its organization, worship, doctrine, mission, and work, with no point of return. Fortunately, these matters have been pre-determined by God's instructions in His Word. A standard supplies our point of return in reference to our relationship with God. We are warned "not to go beyond what is written" (1 Corinthians 4:6).

Delegated Authority

First, all authority resides with God (Genesis 1:1; John 17:1-2). Second, God delegated His authority to His Son, Jesus Christ (Hebrews 1:1-2). Third, Jesus sent the Holy Spirit to guide the apostles into all truth (John 16:13). Fourth, the New Testament writers recorded God's will for man in these "last days" (Christian era) by inspiration (2 Peter 1:21). The New Testament is the final, complete, authoritative, objective body of truth for mankind today (2 Peter 1:3; Galatians 1:6-12; John 12:48). Since the Bible is God's will for mankind, we must open it, read it, search it, meditate upon it, memorize it, and practice it, to receive all the benefits (1 Timothy 4:11-16; James 1:21; Psalm 1:1-2).

God's Word is complete in every way and is the true standard to measure our standing with Him: "All Scripture is breathed out by God and profitable for teaching, for reproof, for correction, and for training in righteousness, that the man of God may be complete, equipped for every good work" (2 Timothy 3:16-17). God has boundaries and we should desire to be found within them: "Everyone who goes on ahead and does not abide in the teaching of Christ, does not have God. Whoever abides in the teaching has both the Father and the Son" (2 John 9).

Our goal should be to go back to the Bible, the Divine standard, in restoring the church as it was purposed originally.

One Faith

"Beloved, although I was very eager to write to you about our common salvation, I found it necessary to write appealing to you to contend for the faith that was once for all delivered to the saints" (Jude 3). Faith used here means the completed gospel, "the doctrine," "the truth," and "the faith." This body of faith is objective and singular (Ephesians 4:5) and references that which is believed. This body of teaching is illustrated throughout the New Testament: "And the word of God continued to increase, and the number of the disciples multiplied greatly in Jerusalem, and a great many of the priests became obedient to the faith" (Acts 6:7). "The high priest accused the disciples: "And look, you have filled Jerusalem with your doctrine" (Acts 5:28).

The faith means the gospel of Christ – the Christian religion (Galatians 1:6-9, 23).

Jude instructs his readers on why Christians must consistently contend for the faith that has been once for all made known. Christians must recognize the need to stand earnestly for the truth (verse 3).

Saints must be aware of, and dedicated to, their spiritual standing with God (verses 1-2), and they must know how to maintain it.

But you, beloved, building yourselves up in your most holy faith and praying in the Holy Spirit, keep yourselves in the love of God, waiting for the mercy of our Lord Jesus Christ that leads to eternal life (verses 20-21).

We are to remember that God has dealt with error many times and is competent to deal with it again:

Now I want to remind you, although you once fully knew it, that Jesus, who saved a people out of the land of Egypt, afterward destroyed those who did not believe. And the angels who did not stay within their own position of authority, but left their proper dwelling, he has kept in eternal chains under gloomy darkness until the judgment of the great day— just as Sodom and Gomorrah and the surrounding cities, which likewise indulged in sexual immorality and pursued unnatural desire, serve as an example by undergoing a punishment of eternal fire (verses 5-7).

We are to remember the promise of God is to be with those who uphold His Will.

It was also about these that Enoch, the seventh from Adam, prophesied, saying, "Behold, the Lord comes with ten thousands of his holy ones, to execute judgment on all and to convict all the ungodly of all their deeds of ungodliness that they have committed in such an ungodly way, and of all the harsh things that ungodly sinners have spoken against him" (verses 14, 15).

We must hold fast the words of Jesus.

But you must remember, beloved, the predictions of the apostles of our Lord Jesus Christ. They said to you, "In the last time there will be scoffers, following their own ungodly passions." It is these who cause divisions, worldly people, devoid of the Spirit (verses 17-19).

We are to assist, if possible, those in error to return to the truth.

And have mercy on those who doubt; save others by snatching them out of the fire; to others show mercy with fear, hating even the garment stained by the flesh (verses 22-23).

We are to commit ourselves in fullness to the care of God.

Now to him who is able to keep you from stumbling and to present you blameless before the presence of his glory with great joy, to the only God, our Savior, through Jesus Christ our Lord, be glory, majesty, dominion, and authority, before all time and now and forever. Amen (verses 24-25).

Directly related to our topic of restoration, the faith must be proclaimed because only those that "continue in the faith" will be saved eternally. Paul exhorted the Christians at Lystra, Iconium, and Antioch to "continue in the faith" (Acts 14:21, 22). The Corinthians were told to "stand firm in the faith" (1 Corinthians 16:13), and to "examine yourselves, to see whether you are in the faith" (2 Corinthians 13:5).

Three Questions

The authority of God was appealed to by the Apostle Paul when writing to the church at Corinth. Divisions were reported to the inspired writer and he wrote to them with authority ("I appeal to you"). A series of three questions getting to the heart of the trouble in the church was presented that was designed to illustrate that all should be united in Christ, acknowledge that Christ died for us

(Romans 5:8) and that we are baptized in His name, i.e. by His authority (Acts 2:38).

"Is Christ divided?"

The first question addressed the disunity that existed in Corinth. "Is Christ divided?" That is a command of Christ: No divisions. That is precisely what He prayed (John 17), and now He commands it.

I appeal to you, brothers, by the name of our Lord Jesus Christ, that all of you agree, and that there be no divisions among you, but that you be united in the same mind and the same judgment. For it has been reported to me by Chloe's people that there is quarreling among you, my brothers. What I mean is that each one of you says, "I follow Paul," or "I follow Apollos," or "I follow Cephas," or "I follow Christ." Is Christ divided? Was Paul crucified for you? Or were you baptized in the name of Paul? (1 Corinthians 1:10-13).

No denominations. Denominationalism is not in the Word that God, the Holy Spirit, and Jesus Christ gave to the world.

Jesus prayed for the unity of all believers, He commands the unity of all believers. Uniting upon the Word of God alone will utterly destroy denominationalism.

"Was Paul crucified for you?"

Jesus came into this world to die for us (Hebrews 2:9). By His death, He shed the blood that cleanses us from our sins (Romans 5:8-10). It was because of His death on the cross, and His resurrection from the dead, that He "was declared to be the Son of God with power" (Romans 1:4).

But why would Paul ask this question? Because some were following Paul. The point is, one does not have the right to follow anyone who was not crucified for them - and only Christ has been crucified for humanity! We must not follow any man over or in the place of Christ.

"Were you baptized into the name of Paul?"

This is a question of authority because it is the action in which we are united with Christ. "Are ye ignorant that all we who were baptized into Christ Jesus were baptized into his death" (Romans 6:3)? Until one is baptized into Christ, he is not "in Christ." There is an inseparable link between baptism and the crucifixion, burial, and resurrection of Christ (Romans 6:1-11).

But the question also pinpoints another important truth: baptism is essentially INTO some name. One does not have the right to wear a name into which he has not been baptized.

Application

The apostle Paul shows that in order for one to be of Paul there are two things that must be necessary. There may be other things, but these are absolutely essential. He says, *"Was Paul crucified for you? Or were you baptized in the name of Paul?"* This demonstrates that in order for a man to be of Paul, or "to belong to Paul," he must first, have Paul crucified for him; and in the second place, he must have been baptized in the name of Paul.

Since Paul had not been crucified for him, and he had not been baptized in the name of Paul, then he had no right to say... "I belong to Paul." The same principle applies to those who said... "I am of Christ," or "I belong to Christ," The same two things must be necessary. In order to belong to Christ, or to be of Christ, Christ must be crucified for you; additionally, you must be baptized in the name of Christ (Matthew 28:18-20; Acts 2:38; 4:12).

Stay with the Truth

When we stay within the truth, we remain within the authority. God's people are to study the truth (2 Timothy 2:15), learn the truth (2 Timothy 3:7), live the truth (Philippians 1:27), and preach the truth (Mark 16:15, 16). "Jesus said, "And ye shall know the truth, and the truth shall make you free" (John 8:32). The Lord's statement should forever settle the matter for all who believe the Bible.

Only by adhering to the Divine standard, the Bible, can we be restored individually and collectively as God's people. The standard, which never changes, provides a point of return and a divine measurement to maintain restoration.

Aspiration

A desire to return to God's way must be in our hearts to accomplish what is necessary to restore original Christianity. Acknowledging a falling away and acquiring the vision to see the standard of authority must be joined with the desire to restore the relationship to God. We make spiritual progress by going back to practicing pure Christianity and living as God has directed in His Word. God will help us in this process: "He fulfills the desire of those who fear him; he also hears their cry and saves them" (Psalm 145:19).

Do we have the desire to honor God by keeping His Word as Paul was to leave this earth and be joined with Christ? "I am hard pressed between the two. My desire is to depart and be with Christ, for that is far better" (Philippians 1:23). Can we say with David: "Delight yourself in the Lord, and he will give you the desires of your heart? Commit your way to the Lord; trust in him, and he will act" (Psalm 37:4-5). May it be said of our daily action: "With my whole heart I seek you; let me not wander from your commandments" (Psalm 119:10)!

"Blessed are those who hunger and thirst for righteousness, for they shall be satisfied" (Matthew 5:6). Do these words of Christ have meaning deep down in our hearts? Do we desire the Word? When the appetite is healthy and we are feeding it the proper diet, the will to return and remain in fellowship with God will be realized. We cannot please God with desire alone: "Desire without knowledge is not good, and whoever makes haste with his feet misses his way" (Proverbs 19:2).

Desire coupled with knowledge and obedience completes the package for the mindset of restoration. "Whoever is of God hears the words of God. The reason why you do not hear them is that you are not of God" (John 8:47). To "hear" the words of God is to "obey" the words of God. "Why do you call me 'Lord, Lord,' and not do what I tell you" (Luke 6:46)?

The Ancient Paths

The desire of man must be in sync with the desire of God. This has always been a challenge to man. There was a continual need for a restoration movement in Israel. The message to conform to the commandments of God came to the children of Israel.

Hear the word of the Lord, O children of Israel, for the Lord has a controversy with the inhabitants of the land. There is no faithfulness or steadfast love, and no knowledge of God in the land...My people are destroyed for lack of knowledge; because you have rejected knowledge, I reject you from being a priest to me. And since you have forgotten the law of your God, I also will forget your children...Return, O Israel, to the Lord your God, for you have stumbled because of your iniquity. Take with you words and return to the Lord; say to him, "Take away all iniquity; accept what is good, and we will pay with bulls the vows of our lips" (Hosea 4:1, 6; 14:1-2).

The prophet Jeremiah was the mouthpiece for God to warn Judah of their sins and to give them a way of escape so they could avoid God's wrath (Jeremiah 6:16). God would allow an enemy force to punish them and bring destruction (6:1-5, 17-30).

Verses ten through fifteen in Jeremiah chapter six, document the sins of the prophets and priests and give insight into their corruptness and rejection of God. We remember how corruption must be present in order for a restoration to occur.

To whom shall I speak and give warning, that they may hear? Behold, their ears are uncircumcised, they cannot listen; behold, the word of the Lord is to them an object of scorn; they take no pleasure in it. Therefore I am full of the wrath of the Lord; I am weary of holding it in. "Pour it out upon the children in the street, and upon the gatherings of young men, also; both husband and wife shall be taken, the elderly and the very aged. Their houses shall be turned over to others, their fields and wives together, for I will stretch out my hand against the inhabitants of the land," declares the Lord. "For from the least to the greatest of them, everyone is greedy for unjust gain; and from prophet to priest, everyone deals falsely. They have healed the wound of my people lightly, saying, 'Peace, peace,' when there is no peace. Were they ashamed when they committed abomination? No, they were not at all ashamed; they did not know how to blush. Therefore they shall fall among those who fall; at the time that I punish them, they shall be overthrown, says the Lord. (Jeremiah 6:10-15).

Jeremiah had been given the wisdom to share with Judah but sadly she would not heed the warnings.

Thus says the Lord: "Stand by the roads, and look, and ask for the ancient paths, where the good way is; and walk in it, and find rest for your souls, But they said, 'We will not walk in it.' "I set watchmen over you, saying, 'Pay attention to the sound of the trumpet!' But they said, 'We will not pay attention'" (Jeremiah 6:16-17).

This passage acknowledges a requirement, a reward, and a refusal.

Requirement

To have gone back to the ancient paths would have been to go back to the covenant which God had revealed in times past, and this would have included the love and morality of the law.

God commanded Judah to be steadfast ("stand") at the crossroads and give attention to ("look") the ancient paths. The word "ask" has the idea embedded in it that means to seek, desire, and investigate with the intention of seeking the correct road. The ancient paths were going back to adherence to God's way in all things. "Where the good way is" reminds us of Psalm 19:7-11:

The law of the Lord is perfect, reviving the soul; the testimony of the Lord is sure, making wise the simple; the precepts of the Lord are right, rejoicing the heart, the commandment of the Lord is pure, enlightening the eyes; the fear of the Lord is clean, enduring forever; the rules of the Lord are true, and righteous altogether. More to be desired are they than gold, even much fine gold; sweeter also than honey and drippings of the honeycomb. Moreover, by them is your servant warned; in keeping them there is great reward.

Reward

The blessings of God in our lives lie in the fact that we must return to His Word and His Way. Jeremiah preached to the people that the reward comes when you "walk in it, and you will find rest for your souls." A life of faithfulness, living and walking in the grace of God with the hope of heaven in our hearts describes the people walking in God's ways. Heaven is our eternal goal and we must stay focused on the big picture and live each day accordingly.

Refusal

The answer of the people was disappointing to God: "But they said, 'We will not walk in it'" (Jeremiah 6:16-17). As humans, we often fail in the decision-making process that is made possible by our free will. Jesus warned us that our choice would determine our eternal address: "Enter by the narrow gate. For the gate is wide and the way is easy that leads to destruction, and those who enter by it are many. For the gate is narrow and the way is hard that leads to life, and those who find it are few" (Matthew 7:13-14). We should say with the Psalmist: "As a deer pants for flowing streams, so pants my soul for you, O God. My soul thirsts for God, for the living God. When shall I come and appear before God? My tears have been my food day and night, while they say to me all the day long, "Where is your God" (Psalm 42:1-3)?

The bold refusal to look for the ancient paths, the good way, and walk in them, was a terrible mistake for Judah and should be a clear lesson for us today.

Desire to Hear and Do

Our Lord demonstrated in word and action the importance of listening to God and then applying the information to His daily lifestyle. He stated His motivation for this practice: "For I have come down from heaven, not to do my own will but the will of him who sent me" (John 6:38). "So Jesus answered them, "My teaching is not mine, but his who sent me" (John 7:16).

The keeping of the commandments of God is linked to our eternal destiny:

And Jesus cried out and said, "Whoever believes in me, believes not in me but in him who sent me. And whoever sees me sees him who sent me. I have come into the world as light, so that whoever believes in me may not remain in darkness. If anyone hears my words and does not keep them, I do not judge him; for I did not come to judge the world but to save the world. The one who rejects me and does not receive my words has a judge; the word that I have spoken will judge him on the last day. For I have not spoken on my own authority, but the Father who sent me has himself given me a commandment—what to say and what to speak (John 12: 44-49).

Our love for God, Christ, and the Holy Spirit (Matthew 22:34-39) should motivate us to faithfully practice the commands of God in every compartment of our lives. "If you keep my command-ments, you will abide in my love, just as I have kept my Father's commandments and abide in his love" (John 15:10).

Separation from God in our individual lives, as well as a depar-ture from God's original intent collectively as God's people, requires a return to God's standard. A dedicated desire is essential to make this happen in any generation.

May we set our minds to obeying the teaching set forth in the New Testament for our lives as Christians and for the body of Christ of which we are members.

Precedent in the Old Testament

Biblical Restorations

Our study of what is inherent in the word "restore" reminds us of the meaning "to bring back to a former or normal condition, as by repairing, rebuilding, or altering" to put the original back in place.

When building a house, blueprints are used which have been prepared by an architect. These blueprints show specifically the dimensions, number of rooms, doors, windows, etc., with the builder being obligated to build the house to the blueprint specifications. As the years pass, modifications are often made to the structure (layout is changed, rooms added, door removed, wall moved, etc.) and the house is not as it was originally. The house may resemble the original but it is different in many aspects. At some point, if someone wants to restore the house to its original design, they must use the original blueprints and remove all additions and modifications, and rebuild according to the original pattern.

The original blueprint, the New Testament, is available and we can restore pure Christianity the way God intended by going back to the perfect source. The Holy Spirit gave us the Word (John 16:13), and we know the seed is the Word of God and when planted and watered will only produce Christians who make up the New Testament church (Mark 13:31).

We find in the Bible numerous examples of individuals as well as God's chosen people collectively needing restoration. The following Old Testament examples serve both of these categories.

Adam and Eve: The Necessity of Restoration Begins

Then the Lord God formed the man of dust from the ground and breathed into his nostrils the breath of life, and the man became a living creature. And the Lord God planted a garden in Eden, in the east, and there he put the man whom he had formed. And out of the ground the Lord God made to spring up every tree that is pleasant to the sight and good for food. The tree of life was in the midst of the garden, and the tree of the knowledge of good and evil...The Lord God took the man and put him in the garden of Eden to work it and keep it. And the Lord God commanded the man, saying, "You may surely eat of every tree of the garden, but of the tree of the knowledge of good and evil you shall not eat, for in the day that you eat of it you shall surely die"...So the Lord God caused a deep sleep to fall upon the man, and while he slept took one of his ribs and closed up its place with flesh. And the rib that the Lord God had taken from the man he made into a woman and brought her to the man (Genesis 2:7-9, 15-17, 21-22).

We begin with life in the Garden of Eden. God's original creation was perfect. Adam and Eve were created as adult humans in a perfect environment, and had full fellowship with God.

God's Creation and Command

When Adam and Eve sinned, the immediate need was restoration. They were now, as all mankind since then, separated from God and lost. The first sin of humanity caused the need for restoration. The story in Genesis chapter three is important to understand for many reasons, including the need to be reconciled to God in a restored fellowship. The words of God to Moses introduce us to God's perfect work in the Garden of Eden. With man and woman now being created in His image, God informs man of some standards…"but of the tree of the knowledge of good and evil you shall not eat, for in the day that you eat of it you shall surely die" (Genesis 2:17). God introduces us to a commandment that prohibits certain activity. We see in this story the beginning of God's pattern that would be different in every age and would involve commandments that called upon man to obey. God's commandments are given for our ultimate good: "And now, Israel, what does the Lord your God require of you, but to fear the Lord your God, to walk in all his ways, to love him, to serve the Lord your God with all your heart and with all your soul, and to keep the commandments and statutes of the Lord, which I am commanding you today for your good" (Deuteronomy 10:13)?

Man's Fall and Disobedience

Now the serpent was more crafty than any other beast of the field that the Lord God had made. He said to the woman, "Did God actually say, 'You shall not eat of any tree in the garden'?" And the woman said to the serpent, "We may eat of the fruit of the trees in the garden, but God said, 'You shall not eat of the fruit of the tree that is in the midst of the garden, neither shall you touch it, lest you die.'" But the serpent said to the woman, "You will not surely die. For God knows that when you eat of it your eyes will be opened, and you will be like God, knowing good and evil." So when the woman saw that the tree was good for food, and that it was a delight to the eyes, and that the tree was to be desired to make one wise, she took of its fruit and ate, and she also gave some to her husband who was with her, and he ate. Then the eyes of both were opened, and they knew that they were naked. And they sewed fig leaves together and made themselves loincloths (3:1-7).

The fall of man and woman began a pattern that is still found in humanity today. "For all that is in the world—the desires of the flesh and the desires of the eyes and pride of life—is not from the Father but is from the world" (1 John 2:16). Satan tempted Eve with these three desires: lust of the flesh, lust of the eyes and the pride of life. "So when the woman saw that the tree was good for food (lust of the flesh), and that it was a delight to the eyes (lust of the eyes), and that the tree was to be desired to make one wise (pride of life), she took of its fruit and ate, and she also gave some to her husband who was with her, and he ate" (Genesis 3:6). Jesus also dealt with these temptations and presented a pattern of how to successfully battle Satan and his deception. Every accountable individual succumbs to temptation from time to time, proving that we all need restoration in our lives because we have violated our walk with God and our Lord Jesus Christ (1 John 1:5-10).

Adam and Eve's breaking of God's commandments in Genesis three set in motion the ultimate struggle every human being since that time would face: sin and how to deal with it.

God embedded the answer to humanity's sin problem in the same section as he revealed the fall. After God spoke to Adam, Eve and the serpent (Satan), He offered the following prophecy: "I will put enmity between you and the woman, and between your offspring and her offspring; he shall bruise your head, and you shall bruise his heel" (Genesis 3:15). The woman's seed represents the people of God who are seeking restoration through the blood of the sacrifice of the Son of the Living God (Romans 5:8), while the serpent's seed represents all those who oppose God and fail to do His Will.

This would serve to produce a restoration of mankind to the God of creation and provide a way to fellowship with the Godhead once again.

Abraham and King Abimelech

In Genesis chapter twenty, Abraham wants all to know that Sarah was his sister, in order to protect him from being killed. King Abimelech took Sarah and had the intention of making her his wife, but God intervened:

> But God came to Abimelech in a dream by night, and said to him, "Indeed you are a dead man because of the woman whom you have taken, for she is a man's wife." But Abimelech had not come near her; and he said, "Lord, will You slay a righteous nation also? Did he not say to me, 'She is my sister'? And she, even she herself said, 'He is my brother.' In the integrity of my heart and innocence of my hands I have done this." And God said to him in a dream, "Yes, I know that you did this in the integrity of your heart. For I also withheld you from sinning against Me; therefore I did not let you touch her. Now therefore, restore the man's wife; for he is a prophet, and he will pray for you and you shall live. But if you do not restore her, know that you shall surely die, you and all who are yours (Genesis 20:3-7, NKJV).

God demanded that Sarah be "restored" to Abraham. The return of Sarah to Abraham represents a case of restoration where a relationship is put back to its original arrangement. King Abimelech was obligated under the command of God to set things back in place as they were before he took Sarah with the intention of her becoming his wife.

This biblical example serves as an individual practicing restoration (to bring back to a former or normal condition, as by repairing, rebuilding, altering, etc.; to put back in a place). God has not left man without direction when he desires restoration whether in the Patriarchal, Mosaic or Christian age.

Josiah: A Noble Restorer

Hezekiah was a noble king of Judah and also a reformer (2 Kings 18:1-7). He was succeeded by his son, Manasseh. Manasseh, who became one of the most infamous kings, was noted for his undoing all his father's work of reformation. He established iniquities and abominations that were shocking and degrading as not before known in Judah (2 Chronicles 33:1-9). After Manasseh's death, Amon, his son, continued his wicked practices (2 Chronicles 33:20-23). Amon was assassinated after two years.

Josiah, his son, inherited a spiritually degenerate kingdom (2 Chronicles 34:1). God's people, Israel, foreshadowed the people of God in the New Testament church.

Josiah was eight years old when he began to reign, and he reigned thirty-one years in Jerusalem. And he did what was right in the eyes of the Lord, and walked in the ways of David his father; and he did not turn aside to the right hand or to the left. For in the eighth year of his reign, while he was yet a boy, he began to seek the God of David his father, and in the twelfth year he began to purge Judah and Jerusalem of the high places, the Asherim, and the carved and the metal images (2 Chronicles 34:1-3).

And they gave it to the workmen who were working in the house of the Lord. And the workmen who were working in the house of the Lord gave it for repairing and restoring the house (34:10).

The Word Discovered

While they were bringing out the money that had been brought into the house of the Lord, Hilkiah the priest found the Book of the Law of the Lord given through Moses. Then Hilkiah answered and said to Shaphan the secretary, "I have found the Book of the Law in the house of the Lord." And Hilkiah gave the book to Shaphan. Shaphan brought the book to the king, and further reported to the king, "All that was committed to your servants they are doing. They have emptied out the money that was found in the house of the Lord and have given it into the hand of the overseers and the workmen (2 Chronicles 34:14-17).

Repairing the temple began in the eighteenth year of Josiah's reign. "Hilkiah the priest found a book of the law of the Lord given by Moses" (2 Chronicles 34:14 -15). God required that the people be taught the law and remember it. Apostasy is caused by people rejecting the laws of God.

Notice the responsibility of the preceding generations. The priests were required to read the law every seven years (Deuteronomy 31:9-11). A boy of seven would hear the law again at 14, 21, 28, 35, 42, etc. The complete law would be read at these times. It is difficult to conceive the ignorance to God's law if this was done. The truth is that failure is found where the Word of God is not known. Apostasy runs rampant where the Scriptures are buried and forgotten.

The Word Read and Believed

Then Shaphan the secretary told the king, "Hilkiah the priest has given me a book." And Shaphan read from it before the king. And when the king heard the words of the Law, he tore his clothes. (34:14-19).

In order for the words of God to have any benefit, they must be read or heard. Josiah had the words of God read to him, and when he heard, he determined to commit to a restoration by removing the corruptions and restoring what pleased God.

The Word Revered as God's Truth

Then the king sent and gathered together all the elders of Judah and Jerusalem. And the king went up to the house of the Lord, with all the men of Judah and the inhabitants of Jerusalem and the priests and the Levites, all the people both great and small. And he read in their hearing all the words of the Book of the Covenant that had been found in the house of the Lord (34:29-30).

When Josiah learned that the book found was really the law of God, he summoned to the temple a great company of priests, prophets, etc. He then read in their ears all the words of the covenant that was found (34:30). He desired them to be instructed in the Lord's ways and obey the law that had been lost and forgotten (34:31). Not only did the king read the law, but made a covenant before the Lord to walk after the Lord, and keep his commandments (2 Chronicles 34:19,21,30-33).

The Word Restored was Followed

And the king stood in his place and made a covenant before the Lord, to walk after the Lord and to keep his commandments and his testimonies and his statutes, with all his heart and all his soul, to perform the words of the covenant that were written in this book (34:29-31).

Josiah did that which was right in the eyes of Jehovah (2 Chronicles 34:2). He serves as a noble example of leading the people back to a right relationship with God. His works were bold as he removed the corruptions and replaced them with what God's Word demanded.

The Word Demanded that Innovations be Removed and Items Neglected be Restored

---

> No Passover like it had been kept in Israel since the days of Samuel the prophet. None of the kings of Israel had kept such a Passover as was kept by Josiah, and the priests and the Levites, and all Judah and Israel who were present, and the inhabitants of Jerusalem. In the eighteenth year of the reign of Josiah this Passover was kept (35:18-19).

They renewed the covenant (2 Chronicles 34:29-33) and they observed the Passover (2 Kings 23:21-27, 2 Chronicles 35).

Josiah had priests and other helpers to remove from the temple vessels made for worship of Baal. He had them burned to ashes and carried away. He purged Judah of images, broke them to pieces and ground them to dust (2 Chronicles 34: 3-7). The measures seemed strong, but God was pleased. His restoration was thorough and effective.

When religion has been corrupted, it has to be restored to its original specifications and intent.

Sometimes those who oppose the restoration principle will argue that we are creating a new church or a new way to worship. Did Josiah create something new or did he restore something old? What was the result when Josiah and the people read and followed the word of God? They restored by removing the unscriptural practices and dedicated themselves to putting back into order what God wanted in the first place.

Ezra and Nehemiah: Restoring the Law of God - Nehemiah 8:1-18

Ezra and Nehemiah were restorers. After returning from Babylonian captivity, the law of God was read to the people. The pattern that God made known through Moses was now being heard again and followed. The book of Nehemiah records the rebuilding of the walls of Jerusalem and the returning of civil authority under Nehemiah. Nehemiah was the leader in the work of rebuilding the walls of the city while Ezra was a scribe, and was a teacher of the law of God and in restoring the temple's worship and service.

Hunger

And all the people gathered as one man into the square before the Water Gate. And they told Ezra the scribe to bring the Book of the Law of Moses that the Lord had commanded Israel. So Ezra the priest brought the Law before the assembly, both men and women and all who could understand what they heard, on the first day of the seventh month (Nehemiah 8:1-2).

As we come to love and revere God, we begin to hunger and thirst for His Word. Peter identified this in the life of a new Christian: "So put away all malice and all deceit and hypocrisy and envy and all slander. Like newborn infants, long for the pure spiritual milk, that by it you may grow up into salvation— if indeed you have tasted that the Lord is good" (1 Peter 2:1-3).

The key is to seek, know and serve the Lord and crave His Word for our lives: "As for you, my son Solomon, know the God of your father, and serve Him with a loyal heart and with a willing mind; for the LORD searches all hearts and understands all the intent of the thoughts. If you seek Him, He will be found by you; but if you forsake Him, He will cast you off forever" (1 Chronicles 28:9).

Hearing

And he read from it facing the square before the Water Gate from early morning until midday, in the presence of the men and the women and those who could understand. And the ears of all the people were attentive to the Book of the Law (Nehemiah 8:3).

A reverence, respect, and response is noted throughout the Scriptures as people hear the words of God. "So those who received his word were baptized, and there were added that day about three thousand souls" (Acts 2:41). "Attentive" here means to perceive, discern, to understand, to know (with the mind), to observe, to mark, to give heed to, to distinguish, to consider, to have discernment, insight, or understanding. Ezra read from the Pentateuch (Genesis - Deuteronomy) for about six hours.

Honor

And Ezra the scribe stood on a wooden platform that they had made for the purpose. And beside him stood Mattithiah, Shema, Anaiah, Uriah, Hilkiah, and Maaseiah on his right hand, and Pedaiah, Mishael, Malchijah, Hashum, Hashbaddanah, Zechariah, and Meshullam on his left hand. And Ezra opened the book in the sight of all the people, for he was above all the people, and as he opened it all the people stood. And Ezra blessed the Lord, the great God, and all the people answered, "Amen, Amen," lifting up their hands. And they bowed their heads and worshiped the Lord with their faces to the ground (Nehemiah 8:4-6).

Reverence for God's Word was exemplified by the people when the book was opened and read before them. In everything we do we are to give glory to God including the reading and listening to His Word. "Therefore, whether you eat or drink, or whatever you do, do all to the glory of God" (1 Corinthians 10:31). The people in Nehemiah's day are an example of accepting the Scripture as God's Words. "And we also thank God constantly for this, that when you received the word of God, which you heard from us, you accepted it not as the word of men but as what it really is, the word of God, which is at work in you believers" (1 Thessalonians 2:13).

Handling

...The Levites, helped the people to understand the Law, while the people remained in their places. They read from the book, from the Law of God, clearly, and they gave the sense, so that the people understood the reading (Nehemiah 8:7-8).

Diligence in handling the Scriptures (2 Timothy 2:15) includes the concept of understanding and making application to our lives. Among the principles of properly handling the Scriptures would be the recognition of the old and new testaments, the authority of Christ, and the living of the Christian life each day, seeking to be more like Christ in all things.

The many statements through the pen of David by inspiration in Psalm 119 give us direction in how to handle God's precious words:

In the way of your testimonies I delight as much as in all riches. I will meditate on your precepts and fix my eyes on your ways. I will delight in your statutes; I will not forget your word. Your testimonies are my delight; they are my counselors. for I find my delight in your commandments, which I love. I will lift up my hands toward your commandments, which I love, and I will meditate on your statutes. Your statutes have been my songs in the house of my sojourning. If your law had not been my delight, I would have perished in my affliction. How sweet are your words to my taste, sweeter than honey to my mouth! Your testimonies are my heritage forever, for they are the joy of my heart. Your promise is well tried, and your servant loves it. Trouble and anguish have found me out, but your commandments are my delight. I rejoice at your word like one who finds great spoil (Psalm 119:14-16, 24, 47-48, 54, 92, 103, 111, 140, 143, 162).

Heeding

On the second day the heads of fathers' houses of all the people, with the priests and the Levites, came together to Ezra the scribe in order to study the words of the Law. And they found it written in the Law that the Lord had commanded by Moses that the people of Israel should dwell in booths during the feast of the seventh month, and that they should proclaim it and publish it in all their towns and in Jerusalem, "Go out to the hills and bring branches of olive, wild olive, myrtle, palm, and other leafy trees to make booths, as it is written." So the people went out and brought them and made booths for themselves, each on his roof, and in their courts and in the courts of the house of God, and in the square at the Water Gate and in the square at the Gate of Ephraim. And all the assembly of those who had returned from the captivity made booths and lived in the booths, for from the days of Jeshua the son of Nun to that day the people of Israel had not done so. And there was very great rejoicing. And day by day, from the first day to the last day, he read from the Book of the Law of God. They kept the feast seven days, and on the eighth day there was a solemn assembly, according to the rule (Nehemiah 8:13-18).

Action on man's part has always been required by God in every age. Listening to His instructions is not sufficient to be pleasing to Him (Genesis 22:15-18).

The Law of Moses revealed through their reading that the Israelites were to live in booths during the feast of the seventh month. This was God's commandment. The Feast of Tabernacles had not been practiced for hundreds of years. This observance had been lost for a long time and it was a necessary work to restore it to its proper place in honoring God and keeping His commandments. It is clear that they went back to the way God had intended ("written in the law," Nehemiah 8:15).

We have to make necessary changes when we find that we are omitting something or that something has been corrupted or changed from the original instructions. The practices that had been lost for hundreds of years were able to be restored, practiced and observed as God intended. Is it an impossible idea to desire to go back to the first century teaching and restore the New Testament church?

Observations

God has always communicated His Will for man in every age.

God has always been a God of a pattern.

The Word of God is the essential key to restoration.

Removing what is not authorized is also necessary to produce the proper restoration and return to God.

A restoration of what is missing is part of the ideal of restoration.

God will not accept just any worship, lifestyle, or teaching.

Man's sin and apostasy imply the concept of restoration. The fall necessitated the need to return to God.

The restoration examples show nothing new was created. The ancient paths were reinstated.

A desire to obey God's Word is always required to fulfill restoration.

Balance is the key (neither to the right hand nor to the left) in order to avoid extremes. God has a standard and we must avoid going too far to the left or the right: "And he did what was right in the eyes of the Lord and walked in all the way of David his father, and he did not turn aside to the right or to the left" (2 Kings 22:2).

God had a plan in place to save man (Genesis 3:15).

Restoration begins with the individual Christian and expands to congregations - each Christian is a member of the body and the body is the church.

Each generation is responsible to God to do His Will.

One generation can change course from a previous one.

People need to be constantly reminded of what the Scriptures teach.

Critics will always be around.

Apostasy - Authority - Aspiration

In each of the cases cited:

First, there was a departure from the word of God. Men had rejected the commandments of God and were no longer worshipping God properly. They had rejected God's plan and God's pattern.

Second, someone found the word of God, read it, and discovered that a departure had occurred. That person decided to follow the word of God rather than the word of man.

Third, the desire to restore the pattern and practices found in the word of God is a necessary part of the process. The people began to worship and serve God according to His commandments. Restoration had occurred.

Warning

It was said of Josiah: "Before him there was no king like him, who turned to the Lord with all his heart and with all his soul and with all his might, according to all the Law of Moses, nor did any like him arise after him" (2 Kings 23:25). Is there any question but that Josiah did the Will of God? Tragically, what he accomplished was short-lived (2 Kings 23:31-37), once again providing another example of the need to maintain a restoration mindset. Man is never satisfied with God's way and will over time drift away from God and His pattern. Man must then be led back to the Scriptures to find what pleases the Father, remove the corruption, restore what is right, and walk in His ways in a balanced way.

Precedent in the New Testament

We are on a Journey. God calls upon each of us to keep the work of restoration alive in ourselves and the congregations in which we serve. It is exciting to be involved in God's work of restoration.

We are simply offering what God desires in principle and practice. As we have studied, the concept is not new or improved, it is simply striving to be what God wants us to be. To the church at Colossae, Paul exhorted them to remove anything that did not fit with Christlike living. This is consistent with the pattern of first removing that which is ungodly:

> Put to death therefore what is earthly in you: sexual immorality, impurity, passion, evil desire, and covetousness, which is idolatry. On account of these the wrath of God is coming. In these you too once walked, when you were living in them. But now you must put them all away: anger, wrath, malice, slander, and obscene talk from your mouth. Do not lie to one another, seeing that you have put off the old self with its practices (Colossians 3:5-9).

We are to add (restore) the qualities and lifestyle required by the Savior:

Put on then, as God's chosen ones, holy and beloved, compassionate hearts, kindness, humility, meekness, and patience, bearing with one another and, if one has a complaint against another, forgiving each other; as the Lord has forgiven you, so you also must forgive. And above all these put on love, which binds everything together in perfect harmony. And let the peace of Christ rule in your hearts, to which indeed you were called in one body. And be thankful. Let the word of Christ dwell in you richly, teaching and admonishing one another in all wisdom, singing psalms and hymns and spiritual songs, with thankfulness in your hearts to God. And whatever you do, in word or deed, do everything in the name of the Lord Jesus, giving thanks to God the Father through him (Colossians 3:12-17).

We do not seek to belittle or look down upon others for their beliefs. Our aim is to be the disciples Christ describes in His Word. The results will be starkly diverse from what we see in the religious world today. Our journey involves opening people's minds and helping to clear the clutter of man's opinions and seek to only practice what God desires.

Where do we go from here?

The procedure in the restoration process involves at least three components. We ask, like Thomas, "how can we know the way" (John 14:5)?

Educating

To begin with, we must be educated in the truth. This requires a lifelong process with a desire to seek and know the truth of God's Word and His Will for our lives. We (the church) must understand who we are and what we believe (1 Peter 3:15), in order to lead others to the saving gospel of Christ. How can we promote and offer something we are not dedicated to and knowledgeable of ourselves?

We have a unique God-given identity: we are undenominational.

We have a responsibility to share our knowledge of God's will for man (Matthew 28:18-20), and allow the truth to lead and guide us in all things.

Engaging

The second component requires practicing our Christianity faithfully.

Know this, my beloved brothers: let every person be quick to hear, slow to speak, slow to anger; for the anger of man does not produce the righteousness of God. Therefore put away all filthiness and rampant wickedness and receive with meekness the implanted word, which is able to save your souls. But be doers of the word, and not hearers only, deceiving yourselves. For if anyone is a hearer of the word and not a doer, he is like a man who looks intently at his natural face in a mirror. For he looks at himself and goes away and at once forgets what he was like. But the one who looks into the perfect law, the law of liberty, and perseveres, being no hearer who forgets but a doer who acts, he will be blessed in his doing. If anyone thinks he is religious and does not bridle his tongue but deceives his heart, this person's religion is worthless. Religion that is pure and undefiled before God the Father is this: to visit orphans and widows in their affliction, and to keep oneself unstained from the world (James 1:19-27).

In this text, James welds together faith and works. It is not sufficient to say we have faith...we must prove it through our works.

In the above reference, "put away" reminds us that sin has to be removed and we must receive the implanted word to prepare us to be doers living out our Christianity. James is clear that if we look into the mirror and forget we end up being deceived and our religion is worthless. On the other hand, we are encouraged that if we are doers we will be blessed and enjoy pure and undefiled spirituality before God. "Why do you call me 'Lord, Lord,' and not do what I tell you?" (Luke 6:46). This is related to Jesus stating: "And he said to all, "If anyone would come after me, let him deny himself and take up his cross daily and follow me" (Luke 9:23).

Restoration is a "doing" principle and can only be successful when we remember that Christ is our pattern (1 Peter 2:21), and we humbly, prayerfully, and scripturally line up in heart, soul, body and mind with God's way for our lives.

Evolving

Restoring original Christianity is an on-going process which is our third component. Each generation must study and determine what is right and seek to put it into practice within the culture they are living. As the biblical examples, illustrations and implications confirm, man is always falling short of God's ideal and maintenance must be continually practiced. This should be evidenced by removing sin and hindrances, and seeking to restore the things which are lacking in our lifestyle, worship, work and service.

Restoring Practices

The restoration principle cannot be limited to just how we worship God, the organizational structure of the church or the plan of salvation. We must be careful to not be short-sighted in our approach to restoring. In the previous sections, we have noted the mandate to remove unscriptural additions and modifications and restore the correct practices and structure as God desires in our current time in history (Christian age).

Realistically, we are acknowledging a mixture of successes and failures in our efforts to restore New Testament Christianity. Jesus issued strong language to the Pharisees when he accused them of missing essential qualities in their lifestyle and religion: "Woe to you, scribes and Pharisees, hypocrites! For you tithe mint and dill and cumin, and have neglected the weightier matters of the law: justice and mercy and faithfulness. These you ought to have done, without neglecting the others. You blind guides, straining out a gnat and swallowing a camel" (Matthew 23:23-24)!

We must not fall short in living like Jesus while thinking doctrinal integrity will be the only criteria in the judgment.

The restoring of New Testament Christianity involves many facets, including:

> The recognition of Christ as the supreme authority in religion (Matthew 28:18; Colossians 3:17).
>
> The acknowledgement of New Testament as only rule of faith and practice (Jude 3).
>
> The proper distinction between the Old and New Testaments (Exodus 34:27-28; Matthew 5:17-18; Colossians 2:14; Hebrews 9:14-17).
>
> The restoring of the New Testament pattern for the ordinances of the church. The essentiality of baptism, the observance of the Lord's Supper every Sunday, and the acknowledgement of Sunday as the Lord's Day.

The term ordinance may seem peculiar to our thinking but it means "a direction or command of an authoritative nature" (*Webster's*, 1015). The church has no ordinances, but Christ has three: (1) Baptism, (2) the Lord's Supper, and (3) the Lord's Day. These three ordinances have great teaching value to the Christian.

> The gospel of Christ has three facts—the death, the burial, and the resurrection of Jesus.

Now I would remind you, brothers, of the gospel I preached to you, which you received, in which you stand, and by which you are being saved, if you hold fast to the word I preached to you—unless you believed in vain. For I delivered to you as of first importance what I also received: that Christ died for our sins in accordance with the Scriptures, that he was buried, that he was raised on the third day in accordance with the Scriptures (1 Corinthians 15:1-4).

Each of the three ordinances of Christ memorializes one or more facts of the gospel.

Paul lists three foundational observances.

The Lord's Supper. Observe first, "Christ died." The Lord's Supper is a memorial and a proclamation of the death of Christ participated in as a sacred and impressive memorial on the first day of the week (Acts 20:7).

Baptism. Observe the second fact of the gospel: Christ was buried. The monument that attests to His burial is baptism. Baptism, while a command, is also a memorial that pictures the death, burial, and resurrection of Jesus. "What shall we say then? Are we to continue in sin that grace may abound? By no means! How can we who died to sin still live in it? Do you not know that all of us who have been baptized into Christ Jesus were baptized into his death? We were buried therefore with him by baptism into death, in order that, just as Christ was raised from the dead by the glory of the Father, we too might walk in newness of life" (Romans 6:1-4). Today, when you witness a scriptural baptism, you have pictured before your very eyes the death, burial, and resurrection of Christ.

The Lord's Day. The third fact of the gospel is the resurrection of Jesus from the dead. The first day of the week, also known as the Lord's Day, is the memorial of the resurrection of Jesus: "Now when he rose early on the first day of the week (Mark 16:9; Psalm 118:22-23). To the Jews the Sabbath, also known as Saturday, was a memorial of the Passover and their passage out of Egypt. To the Christian, the first day of the week, or Sunday, is a memorial of the day Christ was raised from the dead. Each year for fifty-two times, Christians faithful to God's word celebrate the resurrection of Christ (Acts 20:7; 1 Corinthians 16:2;). It is as the apostle John wrote: "I was in the Spirit on the Lord's day" (Revelation 1:10).

Concerning these three ordinances, someone has suggested that (1) baptism is a test of the loyalty of the penitent believer, (2) the Lord's Supper is the test of the loyalty of a Christian, and (3) the Lord's Day is a memorial of the resurrection of Christ.

Pattern of Silence

The silence of the Bible on any given topic often presents challenges to Bible students unless they are equipped to navigate principles of interpretation to make sense of the apparent lack of information. Statements such as: "The Bible doesn't say not to do it," The Bible does not say "Thou shalt not…", are evidence of a lack of understanding how God teaches and authorizes. The question is not: "where does the Bible say not to do it?" The real question is: "where does the Bible authorize or allow it?"

God's Word Is Decisive

What is Written is Authoritative

- And now, O Israel, listen to the statutes and the rules that I am teaching you, and do them, that you may live, and go in and take possession of the land that the Lord, the God of your fathers, is giving you (Deuteronomy 4:1).

- Everything that I command you, you shall be careful to do. You shall not add to it or take from it (Deuteronomy 12:32).

- The secret things belong to the Lord our God, but the things that are revealed belong to us and to our children forever, that we may do all the words of this law (Deuteronomy 29:29).

- But Micaiah said, "As the Lord lives, what the Lord says to me, that I will speak" (1 Kings 22:14).

- That you may learn by us not to go beyond what is written (1 Corinthians 4:6; see also Numbers 24:13).

- And whatever you do, in word or deed, do everything in the name of the Lord Jesus, giving thanks to God the Father through him (Colossians 3:17).

- If anyone speaks, *let him speak* as the oracles of God (1 Peter 4:11, NKJV).

These Scriptures remind us that the Bible authorizes a belief or practice by what it says. We are repeatedly encouraged to listen, and be careful to do everything by the authority of God's Word.

The following Scriptures provide us with a window into how essential it is to do what God says in His Word. Included are also warnings not to do more or less than God prescribes.

- But Balaam answered and said to the servants of Balak, "Though Balak were to give me his house full of silver and gold, I could not go beyond the command of the Lord my God to do less or more" (Numbers 22:18). And the angel of the Lord said to Balaam, "Go with the men, but speak only the word that I tell you." So Balaam went on with the princes of Balak (Numbers 22:35).

Behold, I received a command to bless: he has blessed, and I cannot revoke it. (Numbers 23:20). But Balaam answered Balak, "Did I not tell you, 'All that the Lord says, that I must do'?" (Numbers 23:26).

- But Micaiah said, "As the Lord lives, what the Lord says to me, that I will speak" (1 Kings 22:14).

- Everyone who goes on ahead and does not abide in the teaching of Christ, does not have God. Whoever abides in the teaching has both the Father and the Son. If anyone comes to you and does not bring this teaching, do not receive him into your house or give him any greeting, for whoever greets him takes part in his wicked works (2 John 9-11).

God's Word Is Declared

Prohibitive Arguments From Silence

God presents many warnings throughout His Word that teach mankind to respect His Word and do what it says while also demanding that His silence be respected. The following five examples illustrate how the Scriptures argue from the premise of God's silence forbidding actions contrary (adding to, taking away, or modifying) to His will.

For the sons of Judah have done evil in my sight, declares the Lord. They have set their detestable things in the house that is called by my name, to defile it. And they have built the high places of Topheth, which is in the Valley of the Son of Hinnom, to burn their sons and their daughters in the fire, which I did not command, nor did it come into my mind (Jeremiah 7:30-31).

That which God has not commanded is forbidden: "which I did not command, nor did it come into my mind."

And after there had been much debate, Peter stood up and said to them, "Brothers, you know that in the early days God made a choice among you, that by my mouth the Gentiles should hear the word of the gospel and believe. And God, who knows the heart, bore witness to them, by giving them the Holy Spirit just as he did to us, and he made no distinction between us and them, having cleansed their hearts by faith" (Acts 15:7-9). "Since we have heard that some persons have gone out from us and troubled you with words, unsettling your minds, although we gave them no instructions" (Acts 15:24).

There was no command from God to bind circumcision upon those in Christ: "we gave them no instruction."

For to which of the angels did God ever say, "You are my Son, today I have begotten you"? Or again, "I will be to him a father, and he shall be to me a son" (Hebrews 1:5)?

It is presumptuous of man to speak in God's behalf on a matter He has not spoken: "For to which of the angels did God ever say?"

And to which of the angels has he ever said, "Sit at my right hand until I make your enemies a footstool for your feet" (Hebrews 1:13)?

The same principle is found eight verses later: "And to which of the angels has he ever said."

Now if perfection had been attainable through the Levitical priesthood (for under it the people received the law), what further need would there have been for another priest to arise after the order of Melchizedek, rather than one named after the order of Aaron? For when there is a change in the priesthood, there is necessarily a change in the law as well. For the one of whom these things are spoken belonged to another tribe, from which no one has ever served at the altar. For it is evident that our Lord was descended from Judah, and in connection with that tribe Moses said nothing about priests (Hebrews 7:11-14).

For Jesus to serve as our high priest, the Old Law had to be taken away, for only members of the tribe of Levi could be priests under it. Jesus was of the tribe of Judah. Did God expressly state for Jesus "not to" be a priest while the Law of Moses was still in force? Clearly, the answer is no. Jesus was prohibited from serving as a priest during the Law of Moses because Moses spoke nothing about priests from the tribe of Judah. It was God's silence that prevented Jesus from serving as a priest under Mosaic Law. In order for people to know that priests were allowed from only the tribe of Levi, it was not necessary for Moses to name and specifically exclude every other tribe of Israel. He needed only to specify Levi which serves as a powerful example of God's prohibitive silence. The change in the law (Law of Moses abolished and the Law of Christ brought into force by the death of Christ) enabled Jesus to serve as our great high priest after the order of Melchizedek (Hebrews 7:12).

God's Word Is Developed

God's Commands Both Inclusive and Exclusive

God's commands include what He desires. His commands exclude what He does not desire. When He tells us what is included, He does not have to tell us what is excluded! When we have a specific command from God, we must obey God by accomplishing the command as specified by God. When we have a general command from God, we must employ lawful expediencies to carry out the command.

In every command from God we have generic and specific authority. When God specifies, it is obligatory and must be practiced. God requires us to sing congregationally (Ephesians 5:19; Colossians 3:16) and no other option is specified. Singing is the kind of music God demands. The generic area of a requirement allows options in how to execute what God desires. For example, the words of a song in a songbook or on a screen assist us in all singing the same words together at the same time. This does not interfere with singing one to another. It helps to facilitate it. Adding an instrument to the worship would be violating God's specific command and would be sin. The options chosen cannot disobey another command or principle from God's Word.

Examine the following examples carefully by asking these questions:

What command is present in the passage?

Is it specific?

Is it general? If so, what expedients would be permitted to help fulfill the generic command?

What would be forbidden?

73

Ark

"Make yourself an ark of gopher wood. Make rooms in the ark, and cover it inside and out with pitch" (Genesis 6:14).

When God specified gopher wood, every other kind of wood was excluded. Noah had to employ the specifics of God's command. He had to make lawful choices (i.e., employ lawful expediencies) to fulfill the general aspects of God's command. Noah did not leave anything out or change any of God's commands in building the ark. How do we know this?

"Noah did this; he did all that God commanded him" (Genesis 6:22).

Passover

Your lamb shall be without blemish, a male a year old. You may take it from the sheep or from the goats, and you shall keep it until the fourteenth day of this month, when the whole assembly of the congregation of Israel shall kill their lambs at twilight (Exodus 12:3-13).

God specified the kind of animal to be offered. This excluded any other kind of animal. Because God specified the kind of animal to offer, they had no choice but to offer the specified kind.

Tabernacle

Exodus 25:9, 40; 35:30-35; Acts 7:44; Hebrews 8:5;9:1

In giving Moses the instructions (pattern) on building the tabernacle, God records: "this Moses did; according to all that the Lord commanded him, so he did" (Exodus 40:16). Moses did not deviate from God's pattern in any detail.

Nadab and Abihu

> Now Nadab and Abihu, the sons of Aaron, each took his censer and put fire in it and laid incense on it and offered unauthorized fire before the Lord, which he had not commanded them. And fire came out from before the Lord and consumed them, and they died before the Lord (Leviticus 10:1-2).

When we approach God in worship, we must do only what He has commanded. This was the mistake made by Nadab and Abihu (Leviticus 10:1). When we offer something God has not commanded as is observed in Leviticus 10:3.

- We do not regard Him as holy.
- We do not truly glorify Him.

The fringe on the borders of their garments (Numbers 15:38-40).

God did not state that silence authorizes, and that they could use various colors (their choice), in addition to what he specified (blue).

Moses strikes the rock (Numbers 20:7-11; Exodus 17:6-7; Numbers 20:11-12).

Where God had sanctioned Moses the first time with striking the rock, the second instance God gave him new instructions, which voided out doing it the way he did before.

King Uzziah (2 Chronicles 26:17-19).

Corresponding to the argument from silence regarding men from Judah not serving as priests under the Law of Moses as in Hebrews 7:13-14, here we have Azariah along with eighty priests using the argument from silence to forbid King Uzziah from burning incense in the house of the Lord: "But Azariah the priest went in after him, with eighty priests of the Lord who were men of valor, and they withstood King Uzziah and said to him, "It is not for you, Uzziah, to burn incense to the Lord, but for the priests, the sons of Aaron, who are consecrated to burn incense. Go out of the sanctuary, for you have done wrong, and it will bring you no honor from the Lord God" (2 Chronicles 26:17-18).

Saul (1 Samuel 13:8-14; 15:11; 1:3-4; 1 Kings 3:4; 1 Samuel 13:15-14:3; 10:8; 13:8-11).

"And Samuel said to Saul, "You have done foolishly. You have not kept the command of the Lord your God, with which he commanded you" (1 Samuel 13:13). The Bible records that Saul waited the appointed time of seven days. Consider that Samuel did not say that if I do not come in seven days you can offer, or have someone else to offer, the sacrifices. Samuel was silent on any such permission or authority.

The Ark of the Covenant (1 Samuel 6:19; Numbers 4:5, 15, 20; Exodus 25:12-16; Numbers 7:9; 1 Chronicles 13:7, 9-10; 15:2, 15).

In transporting the ark of the covenant, God specified that it should be conveyed on staves by the priests; He didn't say don't convey the ark on a cart pulled by oxen, so David had it transported on a cart drawn by oxen driven by Uzzah who was not a priest. "And when they came to the threshing floor of Nacon, Uzzah put out his hand to the ark of God and took hold of it, for the oxen stumbled. And the anger of the Lord was kindled against Uzzah, and God struck him down there because of his error, and he died there beside the ark of God" (2 Samuel 6:6-7). The result was death to Uzzah.

David got the point however, when they transported it later; David said that the time before they did not transport it "according to the due order" (I Chronicles 15:13). Uzzah presumed he could touch the ark of the covenant to keep it from falling off the cart, and broke God's commandment. But "he did it because he cared"…"he was sincere"…"his heart was right. This act kindled God's anger and Uzzah was judged by God and immediately struck dead. Was silence restrictive 2 Samuel 6:1-11?

God's Word Is Dependent

Relationship Between the Silence of the Scriptures and Expediency

At this point, we must inject a qualification. When God gives a general command, silence may permit certain expediencies. When God gives a specific command, in order to observe the direct command, there may be certain aids that are expedient that will be utilized in harmony with it. God's desire in no way adds to, takes away from or replaces the specific command.

General authority <u>includes</u> expedients. Specific authority <u>excludes</u> any substitution. An expedient is "useful for effecting a desired result: suited to the circumstances or the occasion: advantageous; convenient." (*Webster's*, 500).

Expedients:

> Must first be lawful (1 Corinthians 6:12; 10:23).
>
> Must not be specified.
>
> Must edify (Romans 14:19; 1 Corinthians 8:1; 10:23-24; 14:26).
>
> Must not offend the conscience of others (Romans 14:20-21, 23; 1 Corinthians 8:7-13; 10:32-33).

> Must not be an addition (Galatians 1:8-9;
> Colossians 3:17; 2 John 9-11).

God requires us to choose the means of accomplishing His general commands. Lawful things are the things which God has authorized (1 Corinthians 9:21; Galatians 6:2; cf. Matthew 21:25; 15:8-9; 1Corinthians 4:6; Colossians 3:17; 2 Timothy 3:16-17; 2 John 9-11). We cannot claim something to be expedient unless we first have a general command from God. Expediencies cannot substitute what has been specifically commanded. To make a substitution, we add to God's word or take away from God's word (Deuteronomy 4:2; Revelation 22:18-19).

Consider the following three examples of required biblical practice and how general and specific authority relate and where expediencies can be utilized.

Baptism Commanded:

- Whoever believes and is baptized will be saved,
  but whoever does not believe will be condemned (Mark 16:16).

- And Jesus came and said to them, "All authority in heaven and on earth has been given to me" (Matthew 28:18).

- We were buried therefore with him by baptism into death, in order that, just as Christ was raised from the dead by the glory of the Father, we too might walk in newness of life. For if we have been united with him in a death like his, we shall certainly be united with him in a resurrection like his. We know that our old self was crucified with him in order that the body of sin might be brought to nothing, so that we would no longer be enslaved to sin (Romans 6:4-6).

- And Peter said to them, "Repent and be baptized every one of you in the name of Jesus Christ for the forgiveness of your sins, and you will receive the gift of the Holy Spirit" (Acts 2:38).

Mandatory components: faith, repentance, immersion in water for the remission of sins.

Expedients: baptistry, a statement made before baptizing.

Absence of authority for sprinkling, pouring, infant baptism.

Place to Worship **Commanded**:

- On the first day of the week, when we were gathered together to break bread, Paul talked with them, intending to depart on the next day, and he prolonged his speech until midnight (Acts 20:7).

- And day by day, attending the temple together and breaking bread in their homes, they received their food with glad and generous hearts (Acts 2:46).

- Not neglecting to meet together, as is the habit of some, but encouraging one another, and all the more as you see the Day drawing near (Hebrews 10:25).

- For, in the first place, when you come together as a church (1 Corinthians 11:18).

Mandatory components: The church is to assemble every first day of the week.

Expedients: Meeting location: rented facility, building, house, tent, purchased building.

Absence of authority for teaching and believing that the meeting place (building) is sacred and that the church is the place, i.e. building. Biblically, the church is the people. Many members make up the one body of Christ, the church (1 Corinthians 12: 12; Ephesians 1:22; Romans 12:4-5).

Singing **Commanded**:

- Addressing one another in psalms and hymns and spiritual songs, singing and making melody to the Lord with your heart (Ephesians 5:19).

- Let the word of Christ dwell in you richly, teaching and admonishing one another in all wisdom, singing psalms and hymns and spiritual songs, with thankfulness in your hearts to God (Colossians 3:16).

Mandatory components: Each member participates in congregational singing. Singing from the heart.

Expedients: Pitch pipe, song leader, songbooks, lyrics on screen. do not replace the specific command but help us fulfill it.

Absence of authority for mechanical instruments of music. Solos, duets, quartets, choruses, etc.

Silence is Restrictive

We are commanded to sing, and no mechanical instrument is allowed. The silence here is also permissive in the realm of using a book or screen for the words to the songs or a pitch pipe to secure the right pitch. These are merely aids whereas an instrument, which is another form of music, would supplant the singing and be unscriptural.

When God specifies what he wants, everything else is excluded. When God gives a specific command, that excludes everything else! To illustrate: When you share your phone number, is it necessary to explain to the other person to use the exact number you gave them and not another combination? For example, if my number is 111-222-3223, am I required to explain that is it not 111-222-3233, etc.? Does the silence of not including a wrong combination warrant you to use one? When a doctor prescribes a specific medicine, is it necessary for them to list all the medicines he/she does not want you to take, along with the specific medicine he/she does want you to take?

Is it not the case that the specific medicine in the prescription excludes every other kind of medicine?

Departures

The Bible predicted men would fall away from the truth: "Now the Spirit expressly says that in later times some will depart from the faith" (1 Timothy 4:1).

When we presume to know more than God and take action beyond the borders of His Word and instructions, then we are committing sin and are found outside of fellowship with Him. What does departing from God do? It...

Displeases God

You shall not add to the word that I command you, nor take from it, that you may keep the commandments of the Lord your God that I command you (Deuteronomy 4:2).

And Samuel said, "Has the Lord as great delight in burnt offerings and sacrifices, as in obeying the voice of the Lord? Behold, to obey is better than sacrifice, and to listen than the fat of rams. For rebellion is as the sin of divination, and presumption is as iniquity and idolatry. Because you have rejected the word of the Lord, he has also rejected you from being king" (1 Samuel 15:22-23).

Dismisses Christ's authority

And Jesus came and said to them, "All authority in heaven and on earth has been given to me. Go therefore and make disciples of all nations, baptizing them in the name of the Father and of the Son and of the Holy Spirit" (Matthew 28:18-19).

Moses said, 'The Lord God will raise up for you a prophet like me from your brothers. You shall listen to him in whatever he tells you. And it shall be that every soul who does not listen to that prophet shall be destroyed from the people' (Acts 3:22-23).

Denies Divine pattern

And see that you make them after the pattern for them, which is being shown you on the mountain (Exodus 25:40).

They serve a copy and shadow of the heavenly things. For when Moses was about to erect the tent, he was instructed by God, saying, "See that you make everything according to the pattern that was shown you on the mountain" (Hebrews 8:5).

Follow the pattern of the sound words that you have heard from me, in the faith and love that are in Christ Jesus (2 Timothy 1:13).

Disaffirms walking by faith

So faith comes from hearing, and hearing through the word of Christ (Romans 10: 17).

...for we walk by faith, not by sight (2 Corinthians 5: 7).

Discredits completion of word

Beloved, although I was very eager to write to you about our common salvation, I found it necessary to write appealing to you to contend for the faith that was once for all delivered to the saints (Jude 3).

I warn everyone who hears the words of the prophecy of this book: if anyone adds to them, God will add to him the plagues described in this book, 19 and if anyone takes away from the words of the book of this prophecy, God will take away his share in the tree of life and in the holy city, which are described in this book (Revelation 22:18-19).

Drives individuals to open doors to innovations

Presumptuous sinning is taking matters into our own hands and daringly acting according to our own dictates, rather than being guided and governed by the precepts of God. A failure to listen to and obey the words of truth from God will result in drifting away from the divine pattern. When one deviation from God's prescribed instructions takes place, another one always follows. "For the time is coming when people will not endure sound teaching, but having itching ears they will accumulate for themselves teachers to suit their own passions, and will turn away from listening to the truth and wander off into myths" (2 Timothy 4:3-4).

Divine Deterrents: Warnings from God to man concerning our handling of the Word of God:

- If Balak should give me his house full of silver and gold, I would not be able to go beyond the word of the Lord, to do either good or bad of my own will. What the Lord speaks, that will I speak (Numbers 24:13)?

- You shall not add to the word that I command you, nor take from it, that you may keep the commandments of the Lord your God that I command you (Deuteronomy 4:2).

- Everything that I command you, you shall be careful to do. You shall not add to it or take from it (Deuteronomy 12:32).

- But the prophet who presumes to speak a word in my name that I have not commanded him to speak, or who speaks in the name of other gods, that same prophet shall die (Deuteronomy 18:20).

- Only be strong and very courageous, being careful to do according to all the law that Moses my servant commanded you. Do not turn from it to the right hand or to the left, that you may have good success wherever you go (Joshua 1:7).

- Every word of God proves true; he is a shield to those who take refuge in him. Do not add to his words, lest he rebuke you and you be found a liar (Proverbs 30:5-6).

- Thus says the Lord of hosts: "Do not listen to the words of the prophets who prophesy to you, filling you with vain hopes. They speak visions of their own minds, not from the mouth of the Lord" (Jeremiah 23:16).

- Behold, I am against the prophets, declares the Lord, who use their tongues and declare, 'declares the Lord' (Jeremiah 23:31).

- But Jesus answered them, "You are wrong, because you know neither the Scriptures nor the power of God (Matthew 22:29).

- Thus making void the word of God by your tradition that you have handed down. And many such things you do (Mark 7:13).

- The one who rejects me and does not receive my words has a judge; the word that I have spoken will judge him on the last day (John 12:48).

- By no means! Let God be true though every one were a liar, as it is written, "That you may be justified in your words, and prevail when you are judged" (Romans 3:4).

- I have applied all these things to myself and Apollos for your benefit, brothers, that you may learn by us not to go beyond what is written, that none of you may be puffed up in favor of one against another (1 Corinthians 4:6).

- But we have renounced disgraceful, underhanded ways. We refuse to practice cunning or to tamper with God's word, but by the open statement of the truth we would commend ourselves to everyone's conscience in the sight of God (2 Corinthians 4:2).

- For we are not, like so many, peddlers of God's word, but as men of sincerity, as commissioned by God, in the sight of God we speak in Christ (2 Corinthians 2:17).

- I am astonished that you are so quickly deserting him who called you in the grace of Christ and are turning to a different gospel— not that there is another one, but there are some who trouble you and want to distort the gospel of Christ. But even if we or an angel from heaven should preach to you a gospel contrary to the one we preached to you, let him be accursed. As we have said before, so now I say again: If anyone is preaching to you a gospel contrary to the one you received, let him be accursed (Galatians 1:6-9).

- As he does in all his letters when he speaks in them of these matters. There are some things in them that are hard to understand, which the ignorant and unstable twist to their own destruction, as they do the other Scriptures (2 Peter 3:16).

- I warn everyone who hears the words of the prophecy of this book: if anyone adds to them, God will add to him the plagues described in this book, and if anyone takes away from the words of the book of this prophecy, God will take away his share in the tree of life and in the holy city, which are described in this book (Revelation 22:18-19).

Strong lessons with judgment and consequences follow situations whenever God's silence has been disrespected. The transgressors are punished:

> Moses and the rock (Numbers 20:7-12): punished by being forbidden from the promised land.
>
> Uzzah and the ark (1 Chronicles 13:9-10): punished by death.
>
> Saul's unlawful sacrifice (1 Samuel 13:1-15); Saul spares King Agag (1 Samuel 15:1-26): punished by being rejected as king.
>
> Nadab and Abihu (Leviticus 10:1-2): punished by death.

Conclusion

There are important lessons that each generation must learn and appreciate. One of those lessons would be one that is as old as mankind. The subject of the silence of the Scriptures and the application of generic and specific authority as presented in God's Word is fundamental when it comes to pleasing God.

Though commands impart obligations, it is important to know that some commands do not contain specific ways they are to be carried out. Some contain required specifics while others do not. With this before us, we can study the Bible and understand it (Ephesians 3:4). God has spoken His will to man, realizing that man; in order to be saved, must reason correctly and determine the way to heaven. Would God give us a revelation that we could not under-stand? No!

May we carry the admonition from God to the Israelites into our approach to His Word today: "And it shall be with him, and he shall read therein all the days of his life: that he may learn to fear the LORD his God, to keep all the words of this law and these statutes, to do them" (Deuteronomy 17:19).

Remember: when God specifies something, everything else is excluded. We cannot add to it, modify it, or take away from His Divine will (Deuteronomy 4:2; Revelation 22:18-19).

Principles to Restore

The Unfinished Restoration

The unfinished restoration must be realized in every generation. Are there any attributes found in the New Testament unaccounted for today in our lives and congregations? Most all would admit that there are areas and practices that are deficient and that we must work to restore them to their proper place in order to be pleasing to God.

Restoring Principles

The attitudes and lifestyle of the child of God must also be renewed and restored in order to be pleasing to our Heavenly Father. The spirit in attitude and actions in each individual Christian and congregation must faithfully apply Biblical truth in each generation. Not only must the doctrine of Christ be restored and maintained, but the spirit of Christianity must be in place in order to be balanced. Josiah set an example of balance and we must do the same.

The following are only a cursory list that need attention today. We must remember that while we may need to work on a specific one, another Christian or congregation may be practicing this well and need to focus on something else spiritually in their on-going quest to restore pure Christianity.

Love

> Love is patient and kind; love does not envy or boast; it is not arrogant or rude. It does not insist on its own way; it is not irritable or resentful; it does not rejoice at wrongdoing, but rejoices with the truth. Love bears all things, believes all things, hopes all things, endures all things. Love never ends (1 Corinthians 13:4-8).

Who would deny the fact that we always have room to improve ourselves in the area of loving one another in the body of Christ? The love chapter directs us in a purposeful, committed, unconditional love. It is active good-will toward others. May we be known as Jesus commands for us to be known to everyone around us as individuals and as congregations (John 13:34-35).

Christ-likeness

God desires that we follow the example of our Lord Jesus Christ in every way, especially in our manner of living each day. Study His life in the gospels and seek to emulate His character in all aspects. We must not fall into the view that only our practices in the church are all that will be judged. God expects the full package: correct doctrine and faithful living. To abide in the Godhead is to abide in the doctrine (2 John 9-11).

Zeal

Zeal (fervor) implies energetic and unflagging pursuit of an aim or devotion to a cause. Does this describe you in your Christianity? Are we guilty of being lethargic in our service? "Do not be slothful in zeal, be fervent in spirit, serve the Lord" (Romans 12:11). We get excited and energized for many events of the world but what about worshiping God? Sharing the gospel? Serving someone in need? Being a neighbor to a stranger? We must be "zealous for good works" (Titus 2:14).

Self-denial, sacrifice and self-control

"If anyone would come after me, let him deny himself and take up his cross and follow me" (Mark 8:34). Self-denial ("deny himself") is the effort to avoid things that would draw us away from God (sinful motives, desires, ambitions, lusts, pride). Self-sacrifice ("take up his cross") involves being willing to suffer now to enjoy unspeakable glory in eternity. Self-control ("follow me") requires complete obedience to the Master and Savior, Jesus Christ. Is this trio of traits found in your character? In your congregation?

Discipline

This practice of the early church (congregational discipline) is almost non-existent today. The culture in which we live, coupled with our fear of being criticized, has caused dysfunction when it comes to administering discipline to unruly members. The discipline of members of the body is a Scriptural command and the Bible has much to say about it (Matthew 18:15-17; Romans 16:17; 1 Corinthians 5; Galatians 6:1; 2 Thessalonians 3:6-15; Titus 3:10; 2 John 9-11; Revelation 2:14-16).

- Now we command you, brothers, in the name of our
  Lord Jesus Christ, that you keep away from
  any brother who is walking in idleness and not in accord
  with the tradition that you received from us…As for
  you, brothers, do not grow weary in doing good. If
  anyone does not obey what we say in this letter, take
  note of that person, and have nothing to do with him,
  that he may be ashamed. Do not regard him as an

enemy, but warn him as a brother (2 Thessalonians 3:6, 13-15).

Scriptural, loving, discipline among the believers is for our good (Acts 5:11).

Deeper knowledge of the Bible

Before one goes into deeper waters of Bible study, a solid foundation must be in place. This foundation must be deep rooted and firm, grounded in the milk of the Word (1 Peter 2:2). The Hebrews writer affirms "Therefore let us leave the elementary doctrine of Christ and go on to maturity..." (Hebrews 6:1), signifying that we must feed on the milk before we are ready for the meat of the Word. Being mature in the Word will keep us from practicing unscriptural things and speaking in unscriptural terms and being tossed about with every false wind of doctrine that comes along. Tragically, there are many among us that are still in infancy when they should be full-grown in their Christianity:

About this we have much to say, and it is hard to explain, since you have become dull of hearing. For though by this time you ought to be teachers, you need someone to teach you again the basic principles of the oracles of God. You need milk, not solid food, for everyone who lives on milk is unskilled in the word of righteousness, since he is a child. But solid food is for the mature, for those who have their powers of discernment trained by constant practice to distinguish good from evil (Hebrews 5:11-14).

Priesthood of all believers

Each individual Christian is responsible before God to offer up worship and praise. No one else can "stand in" for us in our worship, service and work toward God. "But you are a chosen race, a royal priesthood, a holy nation, a people for his own possession, that you may proclaim the excellencies of him who called you out of darkness into his marvelous light" (1 Peter 2:9). We are a "royal priesthood" in the Christian Era. As members of the body, each one has a responsibility to perform their duties and use their God-given abilities for the glory of Christ: "For as in one body we have many members, and the members do not all have the same function, so we, though many, are one body in Christ, and individually members one of another. Having gifts that differ according to the grace given to us, let us use them" (Romans 12:4-8). We must avoid the mentality and practice of leaving serving, giving, visiting, teaching, and all other works in the church at the feet of the minister or to that small group of sacrificing members.

The influence of the clergy versus the ordinary members is strong in the religious world and we must be careful to not elevate a minister's word, prayer, practice, or influence, above anyone else, remembering we are all on equal footing in our standing with God.

Our language

The terminology Christians use must be biblical. The old adage to "call Bible things by Bible names and do Bible things in Bible ways" is simply keeping in step with conforming all our being into God's way of believing and practicing His will. "If anyone speaks, let him speak as the oracles of God" (1 Peter 4:11, NKJV). Have we too lightly brushed aside the need to correct the denominational jargon we sometimes hear from one another. The idea that we are "Church of Christ," or make reference to "Church of Christ" preachers, schools, colleges, doctrine or our congregation as a denomination is unscriptural as well as a deterrent to helping people find pre-denominational Christianity. One that is increasing is the use of "pastor" to refer to gospel preachers. This has no biblical basis but is borrowed from the denominational world. The Elders are the pastors according to New Testament teaching (Ephesians 4:11; Acts 20:28; 1 Peter 5:1-2). Let us be satisfied with using language that is biblical and pleasing to God.

Identity

It is essential that we know what we believe and why we believe it! Many have an "identity crisis" today regarding their faith. They are not sure what they believe and so they attempt to ridicule and argue with individuals and congregations because we believe, worship, and teach according to the New Testament pattern. As we live in and function in this world, identity is important. God has prescribed it that way by making us unique individuals, as well as having a unique body of believers, the Church. Our identity is tied to the following:

The Book (John 17:17; 2 Peter 1:20-21).

The Church (Matthew 16:18; Acts 20:28).

The Name (Acts 4:12; Colossians 3:17).

The Authority (Matthew 28:18).

The Unity (John 17:20-21).

The Salvation (2 Timothy 2:10; Matthew 7:21).

The Worship (Matthew 15:7-9; John 4:24).

The Life (1 Peter 2:21; Philippians 1:27).

The Hope (John 14:3; Revelation 21; 22).

Sacrificial giving

Any examination of the early church and their examples of assisting one another with the world's necessities, will impress upon one the closeness and concern they had for each other. Needs arose among the early Christians because of the length of time many of them had been in Jerusalem for Pentecost. Brethren with the means to help out, gladly sold properties and shared with those in need. This was completely voluntary but also motivated by a strong, deep, abiding love for God and for one another (Acts 2:44-46; 4:32-37; 5:1-11; 6:1-7).

What about today? Do we have such an attachment to "things" that we would not part with them in order to assist benevolently a brother or sister in the Lord? Do you ever hear of a fellow Christian making sacrifices like they did in the 1ˢᵗ Century? It is one thing to give out of our overflow, but it is on another level that we give up or sacrifice something we own for someone else.

We must remember:

1. All you have belongs to God (Psalm 24:1)
2. Your earthly possessions are only temporary (Matthew 6:19-20; 1 Timothy 6:17-19)
3. Giving must come from the heart (Proverbs 22:9)
4. Giving is a matter of choice...not law (Matthew 25:29)
5. Giving is an expression of our love for God (Proverbs 3:9-10)

Leadership

The Eldership is not some sort of "honorary position" given to reward men for their years of hard work, but it is a work in and of itself. Their work is to be confined to the local congregation over which they rule (I Peter 5:2).

The reality is that some churches are dominated by dysfunctional Elderships. The office of the Elder in the local congregation should not function as a board of directors or be led by a Diotrephes (3 John).

Serving as a Shepherd over the flock of God involves several heavy responsibilities that illuminate the need for the Elder/Shepherd to be close to the sheep/members.

> To take heed to themselves and to the flock (Acts 20:28).

> To be men of God's word (Acts 20:32; Titus 1:9).

To be examples to the flock (1 Peter 5:3).

To take the oversight (1 Peter 5:2). To rule well (1 Timothy 5:17).

To feed the flock (Acts 20:28).

To watch for wolves (Acts 20:29-30).

To stop the mouths of vain talkers (Titus 1:11).

To decide differences in the church (Acts 15:6).

To admonish the church (1 Thessalonians 5:12).

To support the weak (Acts 20:35).

To watch for the souls of the church (Hebrews 13:17).

Elders are willing to take my soul into their care: individually. They are willing to take the church into their care: collectively. They spend hours of prayer for the wayward member. They engage in heartbreaking sessions to preserve families. They are involved in hours of talking with lost souls and wayward members. Much time and effort are spent in planning to help the church be most effective. They protect the church. They make sure the members receive a healthy (sound) diet of teaching. They are seldom given gratitude for the office in which they serve and are some of the first (along with ministers) who receive criticism when someone is unhappy.

Evangelistic fervor

First Century examples furnish us evidence that the spreading of the gospel was a mission of the church. Persecution helped distribute the Christians in Jerusalem which produced needed results: "Now those who were scattered went about preaching the word" (Acts 8:4).

We need a clear vision of the mission of the church (Luke 19:10;

24:47). We should know the meaning of personal involvement in the work of the church. We must recognize the value of a soul (Matthew 16:26). We need to seek the proper balance of being in the world without being of the world (1 John 2:15-17).

The gospel must be preached to everyone (Mark 16:15; Colossians 1:23; Romans 10:18). This means that the local congregation must have a "world vision." We must begin in our location and then go into the next town and continue to perpetuate the church. The church is an essential component in the plan of redemption for man. Each congregation is to be self-governing and independent. The obligation is clear from the Scriptures that we as members of the body of Christ are to pray for the expansion of the kingdom, give support through financial means, talents, and time along with encouragement to the work, be an actual part of the planting if possible, and remain balanced remembering to fulfill our current responsibilities to our home congregation.

Commitment

And to the angel of the church in Laodicea write: 'The words of the Amen, the faithful and true witness, the beginning of God's creation. "'I know your works: you are neither cold nor hot. Would that you were either cold or hot! So, because you are lukewarm, and neither hot nor cold, I will spit you out of my mouth"' (Revelation 3:14-16).

"Who cares?" Apathy means without feeling; no passion; without fervent spirit. While members of the body of Christ would never be heard mumbling "who cares," the sentiment is lived out in their actions on an everyday basis. Too many members have a commitment to Christ and His church only when its convenient and doesn't conflict with the ballgames, entertainment, and self-absorption that is easy to fall into in our culture of being too busy.

Disciples of Christ should never exhibit an attitude of apathy when we consider that God has provided our salvation and Christ became the sacrifice for us! Our example: "And they devoted themselves to the apostles' teaching and the fellowship, to the breaking of bread and the prayers" (Acts 2:42).

Power in prayer

Serious, challenging situations face us today that can steal our attention, time, concentration, and many valuable traits that are necessary in keeping us on track on our journey as a Christian.

We need to pray more and make prayer more like it is meant to be. We should seek to be more specific in our prayers. Prayer should have the marks of honesty and intimacy with God. The early church serves us in example:

- Be constant in prayer (Romans 12:12).

- About midnight Paul and Silas were praying and singing hymns to God, and the prisoners were listening to them (Acts 16:25).

- Epaphras, who is one of you, a servant of Christ Jesus, greets you, always struggling on your behalf in his prayers, that you may stand mature and fully assured in all the will of God (Colossians 4:12).

- Therefore, confess your sins to one another and pray for one another, that you may be healed. The prayer of a righteous person has great power as it is working (James 5:16).

Courageous church

- Behold, I am sending you out as sheep in the midst of wolves, so be wise as serpents and innocent as doves (Matthew 10:16).

- Rather, speaking the truth in love, we are to grow up in every way into him who is the head, into Christ (Ephesians 4:15).

Stand up for the unborn, the poor, downtrodden, suffering, persecuted...

Eradicate pet sins

> What sin do you hate to have challenged?
>
> What sin do your thoughts tend to drift to?
>
> What sin has the most power over you?
>
> What sin do you defend?
>
> What sin comes to your heart and mind in times of difficulty?
>
> What pet sin do you need to begin working on now in order to continue being restored in the fellowship of the Father, Son and Holy Spirit?

Being ungrateful, sinful pride, selfishness, a lack of self-control, envy, jealousy, sins of the tongue, (profanity, gossip, lying, unjust criticism, euphemisms, slander), lust, materialism (greed, covetousness), are at the top of the list of sins in our everyday lives that must be acknowledged and repented of in order to maintain a right relationship with God.

"And what more shall I say? For time would fail me to tell of" (Hebrews 11:32), *giving, materialism,* the vanishing of our *missionary fervor,* sins of the tongue (lying, gossip, slander, profanity), pornography, self-centeredness, envy, jealousy, revenge, hypocrisy and many others.

Thankfully, Jesus shed His blood to provide forgiveness of our sins:

For all have sinned and fall short of the glory of God...We know that our old self was crucified with him in order that the body of sin might be brought to nothing, so that we would no longer be enslaved to sin. For one who has died has been set free from sin...For sin will have no dominion over you, since you are not under law but under grace...For the wages of sin is death, but the free gift of God is eternal life in Christ Jesus our Lord (Romans 3:23, 6:6-7, 14, 23).

We seek to restore New Testament Christianity in practice and principle. We cannot afford to ignore one over the other. Consistency demands full attention to restoring our lives and the church to God's standard while continuing to grow spiritually which involves maintenance in our lives to remove and repent of sin and restore the things that are lacking.

Partnership

John chapter seventeen stands as one of the great chapters of the Bible. Within it, we have a prayer of Jesus to God the Father. The prayer of Jesus is that all of His disciples be united. In that Scripture, Jesus prays for Himself (1-5), for His disciples (6-19) and for all believers (20-26).

There are many misunderstandings and misapplications of this prayer. Does Jesus teach through his prayer in John 17 that all religious denominations should be united? Is it implied that doctrine is negotiable? Does it give allowances to wear different names, worship in different ways, be organized differently, and teach a way of salvation that is unbiblical?

Unity denotes "oneness."

The question of "who is a Christian" must be answered biblically in order to be in a saved relationship with God and to be one in fellowship with other believers. The example of King Agrippa illustrates that to fall short of being immersed into Christ for the remission of our sins does not make one a true believer, a Christian, in the eyes of God.

King Agrippa was convinced intellectually that Jesus was the

Messiah. "And Paul said, 'I would to God that not only you, but also all who hear me today, might become both almost and altogether such as I am...' (Acts 26:29, NKJV). The apostle knew "faith only" (mental assent only) would not make Agrippa a Christian. The example of the non-obedience of King Agrippa in Acts 26 is a powerful example of salvation being much more than "faith-alone."

> "For the king, before whom I also speak freely, knows these things; for I am convinced that none of these things escapes his attention, since this thing was not done in a corner. King Agrippa, do you believe the prophets? I know that you do believe." Then Agrippa said to Paul, "You almost persuade me to become a Christian." And Paul said, "I would to God that not only you, but also all who hear me today, might become both almost and altogether such as I am, except for these chains" (Acts 26:26-29, NKJV).

Paul cited that Agrippa was a believer in the sense that he acknowledged and was aware of the prophets and what had happened with the death and resurrection of Christ and the spread of Christianity. Agrippa believed Paul's words, but was not obedient to the gospel. Many would assume Agrippa was a Christian because he believed the Scriptures. Even Agrippa realized he was not a Christian and Paul seconded the fact that he would like to have seen Agrippa become as he is (a Christian) without being imprisoned (in "chains").

Desire Unity

> I do not ask for these only, but also for those who will believe in me through their word, that they may all be one, just as you, Father, are in me, and I in you, that they also may be in us, so that the world may believe that you have sent me. The

glory that you have given me I have given to them, that they may be one even as we are one, I in them and you in me, that they may become perfectly one, so that the world may know that you sent me and loved them even as you loved me (John 17:20-23).

In this insightful prayer of our Lord to His Father in heaven, we see prayer to God (Matthew 6:9). Jesus prays for His disciples (17:20-21). Our Lord prays for there to be unity in truth and for His followers to be one.

- And they devoted themselves to the apostles' teaching and the fellowship, to the breaking of bread and the prayers. And awe came upon every soul, and many wonders and signs were being done through the apostles (Acts 2:42).

- Can anyone withhold water for baptizing these people, who have received the Holy Spirit just as we have?" And he commanded them to be baptized in the name of Jesus Christ. Then they asked him to remain for some days (Acts 10:47-48).

- But now in Christ Jesus you who once were far off have been brought near by the blood of Christ. For he himself is our peace, who has made us both one and has broken down in his flesh the dividing wall of hostility by abolishing the law of commandments expressed in ordinances, that he might create in himself one new man in place of the two, so making peace, and might reconcile us both to God in one body through the cross, thereby killing the hostility (Ephesians 2:13-16).

- To equip the saints for the work of ministry, for building up the body of Christ, until we all attain to the unity of

the faith and of the knowledge of the Son of God, to
mature manhood, to the measure of the stature of the
fullness of Christ, so that we may no longer be
children, tossed to and fro by the waves and carried
about by every wind of doctrine, by human cunning, by
craftiness in deceitful schemes. Rather, speaking the truth
in love, we are to grow up in every way into him who
is the head, into Christ, from whom the whole body,
joined and held together by every joint with which it is
equipped, when each part is working properly, makes the
body grow so that it builds itself up in love (Ephesians
4:12-16).

We should observe how the ones who obeyed the gospel on
Pentecost were united in Christ and this was evident in their daily
lifestyle and practices. When Cornelius and his household were
taught the gospel by Peter, they did the same thing as those on
Pentecost in order to become one with Christ and fellow believers.
When Paul wrote the Ephesian brethren, he reminded them of how
they were one in Christ and how the cross brought both Jew and
Gentile together, representing the unity ("There is neither Jew nor
Greek, there is neither slave nor free, there is no male and female,
for you are all one in Christ Jesus," Galatians 3:28) of everyone, no
matter their background, nationality, gender, education, financial
standing, or any differential quality.

Demand Unity Based Upon the Word

The unity Jesus prayed for must be upon His Word. This is
evidenced in the following references:

- I have manifested your name to the people whom you
  gave me out of the world. Yours they were, and you gave
  them to me, and they have kept your word (John 17:6).

- For I have given them the words that you gave me, and they have received them and have come to know in truth that I came from you; and they have believed that you sent me (John 17:8).

- And I am no longer in the world, but they are in the world, and I am coming to you. Holy Father, keep them in your name, which you have given me, that they may be one, even as we are one (John 17:11).

- I have given them your word, and the world has hated them because they are not of the world, just as I am not of the world (John 17:14).

- Sanctify them in the truth; your word is truth (John 17:17).

- And for their sake I consecrate myself, that they also may be sanctified in truth (John 17:19).

- I do not ask for these only, but also for those who will believe in me through their word, that they may all be one, just as you, Father, are in me, and I in you, that they also may be in us, so that the world may believe that you have sent me (John 17:20-21).

The unity for which Christ prayed to the Father is based upon the whole truth that has been given once for all (Jude 3).

The Divine Platform of Unity

I therefore, a prisoner for the Lord, urge you to walk in a manner worthy of the calling to which you have been called, with all humility and gentleness, with patience, bearing with one another in love, eager to maintain the unity of the Spirit in the bond of peace. There is one body and one Spirit—just as you were called to the one hope that belongs to your call —one Lord, one faith, one baptism, one God and Father of all, who is over all and through all and in all (Ephesians 4:1-6).

There are two sets of keys in this classic text. In order to have our religious practices in the proper order and place, the first set of keys addresses our hearts which must be attuned to what God desires. Our Christian growth and maturity will help set up the playing field for the second set of keys, putting the right doctrine in place.

In the first set of keys, we find *humility*. "Do not be haughty, but associate with the lowly. Never be wise in your own sight" (Romans 12:16). The next quality key is *gentleness*. The idea behind this word is showing patience, being gentle, offering an element of long-suffering (Matthew 5:5). *Patience* is next in our Christian growth. *Bearing with one another in love* comes next. Always being "eager to maintain the unity of the Spirit" will do our part in helping all disciples of Jesus to stand as one in the teaching of the Spirit (John 17:20). The gospel is referred to as a gospel of peace (Romans 10:15) and we are to teach and live "in the bond of peace."

The second set of keys is to the oneness of the Doctrine of Christ. The following are from Ephesians 4:4-6:

> Unity of Organization: One Body.
>
> Unity of Revelation: One Spirit.
>
> Unity of Aim: One Hope.
>
> Unity of Authority: One Lord.
>
> Unity of Doctrine: One Faith.
>
> Unity of Practice: One Baptism.
>
> Unity of Worship: One God.

Many biblical beliefs and practices found in the New Testament fall into each of these categories of unity.

How often do we hear that one faith is as good as another? How about one church? What about one baptism being as good as another? One name as good as another? The Bible regards division as sinful (1 Corinthians 1:10; Ephesians 1:10). However, not all division is sinful. There may be a situation where the faithful are forced to leave a congregation, where unscriptural activities or innovations are being practiced. The concept of one thing being as good as another is not of God, but originates with man. It is the attitude that says "I'm okay, you're okay. We have differences, let's let everything that divides us be set aside and let's have fellowship." Unity in truth forbids unity in false doctrine or unscriptural practices. Only those who have been immersed for the remission of sins can scripturally be in fellowship with each other.

Unity in Christ

The desire of God and the prayer of Christ is that Christians be united and "think and act as if you all had the same mind" (1 Corinthians 1:10, NLV). The following points provide us a picture of the unity which Scripture demands.

Prophesied

The unity in Christ for all believers (1 Corinthians 1:10) is outlined in the New Testament. It was prophesied, "And I have other sheep that are not of this fold. I must bring them also, and they will listen to my voice. So there will be one flock, one shepherd" (John 10:16). It was promised by the Holy Spirit,

---

I still have many things to say to you, but you cannot bear them now. When the Spirit of truth comes, he will guide you into all the truth, for he will not speak on his own authority, but whatever he hears he will speak, and he will declare to you the things that are to come (John 16:12-13. See also, John 17:20-23).

Perfect

This unity was made possible by the perfect sacrifice of the Son of God,

> But now in Christ Jesus you who once were far off have been brought near by the blood of Christ. For he himself is our peace, who has made us both one and has broken down in his flesh the dividing wall of hostility by abolishing the law of commandments expressed in ordinances, that he might create in himself one new man in place of the two, so making peace, and might reconcile us both to God in one body through the cross, thereby killing the hostility (Ephesians 2:13-16).

Promised

The Holy Spirit predicted the unity for which Jesus died. Christ left the disciples with the promise of the Comforter who would guide them into all truth. This truth would provide the boundaries of the fellowship in Christ.

> These things I have spoken to you while I am still with you. But the Helper, the Holy Spirit, whom the Father will send in my name, he will teach you all things and bring to your remembrance all that I have said to you (John 14:25-26). I still have many things to say to you, but you cannot bear them now. When the Spirit of truth comes, he will guide you into all the truth, for he will not speak on his own authority, but whatever he hears he will speak, and he will declare to you the things that are to come. He will glorify me, for he will take what is mine and declare it to you. All that the Father

has is mine; therefore I said that he will take what is mine and declare it to you (John 16:12-15).

Place of Safety

The unity Christ provides is in the body, the church, to which believers (those who repent and are baptized for the remission of their sins) are added by the Lord,

Now when they heard this they were cut to the heart, and said to Peter and the rest of the apostles, "Brothers, what shall we do?" And Peter said to them, "Repent and be baptized every one of you in the name of Jesus Christ for the forgiveness of your sins, and you will receive the gift of the Holy Spirit. For the promise is for you and for your children and for all who are far off, everyone whom the Lord our God calls to himself." And with many other words he bore witness and continued to exhort them, saying, "Save yourselves from this crooked generation." So those who received his word were baptized, and there were added that day about three thousand souls… praising God and having favor with all the people. And the Lord added to their number day by day those who were being saved (Acts 2:37-41,47).

Jesus was praying for those who would be found in Him. He was not praying about unity among the denominational churches (of men) who are divided by a multiplicity of false doctrines and practices contrary to the Scriptures.

The Corinthian church was established with the preaching of the gospel by Paul: "Crispus, the ruler of the synagogue, believed in the Lord, together with his entire household. And many of the Corinthians hearing Paul believed and were baptized" (Acts 18:8).

The unity defined by God is illustrated by the following references where being one with Christ biblically is by being immersed into Christ for the remission of our sins and being added to the body by the Lord:

And such were some of you. But you were washed, you were sanctified, you were justified in the name of the Lord Jesus Christ and by the Spirit of our God...Is Christ divided? Was Paul crucified for you? Or were you baptized in the name of Paul?...For just as the body is one and has many members, and all the members of the body, though many, are one body, so it is with Christ. For in one Spirit we were all baptized into one body—Jews or Greeks, slaves or free— and all were made to drink of one Spirit (1 Corinthians 6:11; 1:13; 12:12-13).

This unity was not based upon a compromise of the truth. It was not an ecumenical (a disregarding of biblical doctrine in order to accept and fellowship other groups in their error) "unity in diversity" of a multiplicity of doctrines and practices originated by men. It was not a "core gospel" concept that minimizes essential doctrinal practices and beliefs.

The biblical framework for restoring man to God and being the church, in the present generation requires maintaining the unity for which Jesus prayed.

The Old Testament teaches: "Behold, how good and pleasant it is when brothers dwell in unity!" (Psalm 133:1), and the New Testament continues the admonition, "Now the full number of those who believed were of one heart and soul..." (Acts 4:32). The inspired record of counsel to New Testament churches highlights the oneness that was to exist among those in Christ: "Complete my joy by being of the same mind, having the same love, being in full accord and of one mind" (Philippians 2:2).

May every soul found in Christ and the New Testament church plead, strive, desire, work, and pray for unity with each other and among congregations restoring New Testament Christianity.

Conclusion

A Scriptural Plea

As we have briefly surveyed, the concept of "restore" is thoroughly biblical. We are called upon to recognize the pre-eminence of Christ in all things (Colossians 1:18). Seeing that the seed is the word of God (Luke 8:11), and the church is produced when this word is preached (Acts 2:38, 47), we must conclude that the church that Jesus established can be produced in every generation, or place, when the Word of God is faithfully preached and obeyed!

We have surveyed Old Testament examples of Adam and Eve, Abraham, Josiah, Ezra and Nehemiah, where we have implications and detailed examples of restoring things back to God's desired specifications.

In the New Testament the restoration mandate seeks to maintain unity with God and all those who have been immersed in the name of Christ for the remission of our sins and who are striving to be the New Testament church. Unity is desired, indeed our Lord prayed for it, but it must come with a total adherence to every precept of God. Not one biblical precept may be compromised if we are to continue to be the church of Christ, existing according to God's pattern.

A Return to God

Departures imply that a standard exists and must be returned to if one is concerned about authentic restoration.

The way back to God requires education in His Word as to our identity. We must engage and practice our faith in order to abide in a faithful relationship to God. In our study, we advanced the point of continuing and maintaining the restoration ideal.

A Recognition of Divine Authority

Authority is the power to command what is right and lawful. Its influence reaches into the very core of who we are and what we believe.

Being dedicated to the Bible as our only rule of faith and practice is necessary in order to remain within the authority of Christ. "We must obey God rather than man" (Acts 5:29), brings the issue of authority to the forefront of all that we believe and practice. The Bible and the Bible alone is all sufficient in matters of faith and life.

We must be a committed people. Paul held up the Macedonians who: "gave themselves first to the Lord and then by the will of God to us" (2 Corinthians 8:5).

Identity

It is of no little significance that Paul included why Timothy was being sent to the Corinthians: "to remind you of my ways in Christ, as I teach them everywhere in every church" (1 Corinthians 4:17). A consistent teaching based upon the "one faith" that was "delivered to the saints" (Jude 3) will produce the same beliefs and practices in every place in every generation.

The restored church will have certain identifying characteristics. We must recognize that the one church that Jesus spoke of is His only church (Matthew 16:18). Wearing the name of Christ in being known only as a Christian only (Acts 11:26), honors the one who died for us and we in turn constitute the churches of Christ

(Romans 16:16). Christ is the head of the body and has all authority in His church (Matthew 28:18).

Christ is our only creed ("Creed" is of Latin origin: "Credo" which means: "I believe"). "For I know whom I have believed" (2 Timothy 1:12).

> No creed but Christ.
>
> No law but the Lord's.
>
> No book but the Bible.
>
> No name but the Master's.

The restoration of Jesus Christ to His proper place in the church and in our lives is required.

The Lord's church has been restored to the New Testament pattern, but the principles of the restoration movement must continue to be maintained. Where there are departures (1 Timothy 4:1), there must be restoration.

The church that we read about in the Scriptures, has a second side (ourselves - humanity) that needs constant maintenance and attention because it drifts away from God's plan and ends up disrespecting God and discarding His Word. The end result is that we need to come back to God as individuals and as the church and restore the practices and principles to His Will in order to be right with Him again. The first side (divine) of the church is fixed and perfect and must be implemented and maintained, needing no revision, human addition, or subtraction. (God has revealed through His Word the characteristics and identifying marks of the church). The human side is susceptible to sin and error but can bring glory to God through repentance and restoration.

A return to the divine ideal must be our goal as we commit to God and seek to return in every way to Him.

Bibliography

Arndt, William, et al., *A Greek-English Lexicon of the New Testament and Other Early Christian Literature* (Chicago: University of Chicago Press, 2000).

Brauer, Jerald C. Ed., *The Westminster Dictionary of Church History* (Philadelphia: The Westminster Press, 1971).

Holy Bible: New Living Translation. Carol Stream, IL: Tyndale House Publishers, 2013.

Mather, George A. and Larry A. Nichols, *Dictionary Of Cults, Sects, Religions And The Occult* (Grand Rapids: Zondervan, 1993).

The Holy Bible: English Standard Version. Wheaton, IL: Crossway Bibles, 2016.

The New King James Version. Nashville: Thomas Nelson, 1982.

Webster's New World College Dictionary, Fourth Edition, Cleveland: Wiley Publishing, Inc. 2010.

Also by Steve A. Miller

Between Sundays

Christianity is to be lived out between Sundays. It is a lifestyle and a worldview. Disciples of the Master Teacher, Jesus Christ live and function in a world that is complacent with regard to serving our Lord with all of our being.

The thirteen chapters in *Between Sundays* serve to remind us that we are called to live our lives daily in submission and obedience to Christ in every way, all the time. Christians do not take vacations from their faith.

Along The Beam

available at

Along the Beam: Living the Biblical Worldview, seeks to understand God's way of seeing the true purpose for our existence, our beliefs, and our lifestyle, by seeing and interpreting everything through the lens of Christ. The concept of biblical worldview is to do the will of God in all situations.

Made in the USA
Columbia, SC
23 April 2024

34467181R00075